Praise for the seco
The Financial Tir
Corporate Valuation

'This book provides an accessible and informative entry point to the vast topic of valuation. The book covers mechanics as well as how value is linked to intangibles, growth opportunities and industry structure, all the way providing clear examples of every key idea. The authors understand value: they know what is useful, what is practical and what is critical, and give any reader great guidance to the challenge of getting values right.'

Bo Becker, *Assistant Professor of Business Administration at Harvard Business School*

'If you can envision the future value of a company you are a winner. Make this comprehensive and diligent book on corporate valuation your companion pursuing transactions and you will succeed.'

Hans Otterling, *General Partner, Northzone Ventures, founder Streamserve & Waymaker*

'Both in my previous position as an investment banker and today as an investor in high growth technology companies, corporate valuation has been a most critical subject. *The Financial Times Guide to Corporate Valuation* serves as the perfect introduction to the subject and I recommend it to entrepreneurs as well as fellow private investors.'

Carl Palmstierna, *former partner at Goldman Sachs, full time private investor*

'Not only will this book provide you with the basic understanding of corporate valuation, it also gives you an interesting insight into non-operational challenges that companies will face. And it does it all in an unexpectedly efficient and reader friendly manner. If you want to learn the basics and only have a few hours to spare, invest them into reading this book!'

Daniel Hummel, *Global Head of Corporate Finance, Swedbank Large Corporates & Institutions*

'A handy, accessible and well-written guide to valuation. The authors manage to capture the reader with high-level synthesis as well as more detailed insights in a great way.'

Anna Storåkers, *Head of Group Strategy & Corporate Development, Nordea Bank AB*

FINANCIAL TIMES

In an increasingly competitive world, we believe it's quality of thinking that will give you the edge – an idea that opens new doors, a technique that solves a problem, or an insight that simply makes sense of it all. The more you know, the smarter and faster you can go.

That's why we work with the best minds in business and finance to bring cutting-edge thinking and best learning practice to a global market.

Under a range of leading imprints, including *Financial Times Prentice Hall*, we create world-class print publications and electronic products bringing our readers knowledge, skills and understanding, which can be applied whether studying or at work.

To find out more about Pearson Education publications, or tell us about the books you'd like to find, you can visit us at **www.pearsoned.co.uk**

2

Presentation of model company

Throughout the book, we will use practical examples in order to explain the various valuation models as simply and as practically as possible. In the examples we will, where suitable, use Mobitronics,[1] a mobile operator based in Benelux, as a model company. In this chapter, we introduce and describe Mobitronics (see Table 2.1).

Mobitronics was founded in 1992 with the aim of establishing itself as an operator in the fast-growing segment of mobile telephony. Today, almost 20 years later, Mobitronics has an annual turnover of €4,640m and a market share of about 22 per cent in Benelux. The market has developed favourably over a number of years and Mobitronics has an impressive customer base, the majority of which are corporate clients. The company has 4,550 employees. Mobitronics has been public for four years and investment bank analysts generally hold the company and its prospects in high esteem. The company is comfortably profitable, sporting earnings before interest, taxes, depreciation and amortization (EBITDA) margins of 44.3 per cent combined with high sustainable growth, low financial risk and stable and financially robust owners.

Mobitronics has three principal products within the mobile telecom industry, namely mobile subscriptions, prepaid phone cards and mobile broadband subscription. The company has employed a differentiation strategy of providing a more complete service package to its customers and thereby increasing the revenue per customer. The strategy has been successful and Mobitronics has higher average revenue per user (ARPU) than its competitors.

---

[1] Mobitronics is a purely fictional company and any possible similarity to a real company and/or real people is entirely coincidental.

■ **Chapter 5**: An in-depth presentation of ratio-based valuations with explanations and formulas for the most common valuation ratios.

■ **Chapter 6**: An in-depth presentation of the McKinsey version of a discounted cash flow (DCF) model and a technique to check your valuation results using mathematical relationships between different valuation models.

■ **Chapter 7**: A discussion of corporate value creation, financial and operative value drivers and presentation of a structured technique, a framework for analyzing the company's underlying business and its environment. This will give you an understanding of the importance of the assumptions underlying the valuation models and the tools to make these assumptions as accurate as possible.

■ **Chapter 8**: A complete valuation, step by step, of our example company Mobitronics, from the underlying analysis to the company's final value, calculated using the frameworks presented in Chapters 5, 6 and 7.

■ **Chapter 9**: Presentation of a management framework focused on creating shareholder value called value-based managent (VBM).

Before we go any further, let us stress that company valuation is not an exact science. No matter who does the valuation, it will always be a function of the valuer's views and beliefs. For this reason it is important to keep the following points in mind:

■ All company valuations are subjective, not objective mathematics. Valuation models are completely dependent on the data inputs and these are in turn based on the valuer's opinions regarding the company/industry/economy.

■ Different parties often have different goals with the corporate valuation – usually there are at least two parties in every valuation situation, often with diametrically opposed interests.

■ The arguments behind your valuation are central – when using the different valuation models presented in this book, you can arrive at whatever value you wish, depending on what inputs you use. Consequently, you must be able to motivate the numbers you use and the assumptions they are based on.

In the next chapter we will introduce Mobitronics, a model company we will be using where appropriate throughout the book.

Why is it so important to understand corporate valuation and the value creation process? Well, firstly because no other measure can indicate as completely the current status as well as future prospects of a company. Secondly, only when understanding valuation can you understand how to maximize the value of your company. Strategies to maximize value without the required knowledge about valuation tend to have less potential for value creation. Thirdly, the development of the value of the company is the best long-term measure of how good a job the present management is doing. Finally, in a company with many shareholders, the owners usually have at least one common goal and that is maximizing the value of the shares. It is important then that all parties agree on how value is measured and how to maximize it.

This book is for readers who would like to understand the topic of corporate valuation and for those who want to know how to work to maximize the value of a business. It is an introduction to corporate valuation for everyone from finance professionals, top management, business owners to business school students. The objective is to give the reader a practical introduction to the subject of corporate valuation and a framework to use with investors, managers, employees or board members.

> This book is an introduction to the topic of corporate valuation and understanding how to maximize the value of a business

As the book's authors are practitioners, rather than theorists, we are aiming mainly at those who need an understanding of the basic principles of corporate valuation rather than those who wish to gain a complete theoretical knowledge.

In addition, to give you the essentials of corporate valuation, the book provides detailed presentations of the two most popular valuation frameworks – ratio-based valuation and the discounted cash flow (DCF) model. This will be done through a structured presentation divided into the following eight chapters:

- **Chapter 2**: Presentation of a fictional company, Mobitronics, which we will use as an example to illustrate various valuation scenarios where appropriate throughout the book.

- **Chapter 3**: Examples of typical situations where corporate valuations are needed and arguments for choosing a certain model in a given situation.

- **Chapter 4**: An overview of the most common corporate valuation models and techniques.

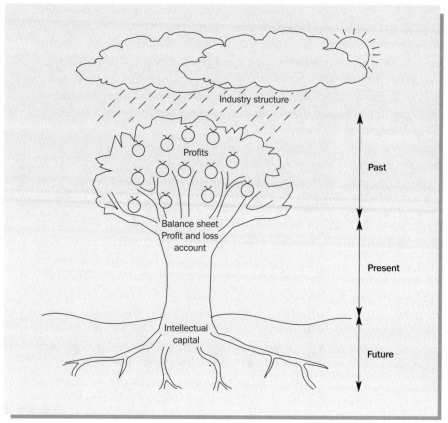

Industry structure

Profits

Balance sheet
Profit and loss
account

Intellectual
capital

Past

Present

Future

Figure 1.1 Tree analogy

An analysis of a company and its value cannot rely solely on analyzing the present and historical balance sheets and profit and loss accounts. These only describe the past up to the present. In order to gain insight into the company's future financial performance, we must also analyze the company's root system, its internal resources or intellectual capital, and its environment – in effect the structure of the industry in which the company operates.

As mentioned above, and as we will show throughout the book, the company's future financial performance is of primary interest when valuing a company, and the past (for example, last year's financial data) is only interesting as a guideline for forecasting the future.

So, to conclude, the aim of corporate valuation is to make your own opinion of the future profit- and cash-generating capabilities of the company and based on that decide what you are willing to pay to take part of it.

corporate value. Pension and hedge funds, investment companies and wealthy individuals now enter company boardrooms with a mission: they are no longer simply selling their shares when dissatisfied with returns, but instead arguing for altered company strategies aimed at maximizing and protecting the value of their shares. The implication for companies is that it is no longer enough to satisfy the customer; a company must also prove itself in the capital markets and management must show it is capable of maximizing company value.

The corporate world has become more dynamic. Mergers, acquisitions, divestitures and corporate takeovers are an increasingly important part of a day's work for many senior managers. Put simply, if a manager does not effectively work to maximize the value of a company, then the chances are that he or she will be replaced or that the company will become the target of a takeover. In fact, maximizing company value and shareholder wealth is increasingly the most important task facing today's managers.

> In fact, maximizing company value and shareholder wealth is increasingly the most important task facing present-day managers

Since the beginning of the 1990s the focus on generating shareholder value has spread like a gospel at business schools all over the world. Now, two decades later, investors from San Diego to Seoul and from Helsinki to Johannesburg steer investment decisions by using valuation methods that capture shareholder value. This is why it is imperative to understand how corporate value is measured. If you are not clear on how markets measure value, you cannot work effectively to maximize it. This applies to all companies – large and small, private and public, new and old.

So what is corporate valuation all about? Let us use an analogy and compare a company to a fruit tree (Figure 1.1). Fruit on any tree is largely the result of past existence. This holds for the profits a company produces as well. This result, or fruit, provides an indication of the tree's health at a particular moment in time, where fruit, like profits, is the visible reward of the past season's endeavours.

> When you buy a company, you buy what is and what is to come and not what has passed

Similarly, compare the branches and the trunk to a company's balance sheet and profit and loss account. These reflect the company's past and present health. But this picture is incomplete without an indication of the tree's ability to produce fruit in the future, that is to say future profits or positive cash flow for the company.

1

Introduction

When writing this book, we seem to have just exited the worst financial crisis since the 1930s. It is not clear how it will all end and if it really is over. New clouds on the capital markets horizon involve debt defaults of southern European countries and gargantuan deficits in the US and UK. Even capitalism, until recently at its peak of global reputation, has come under unusual pressure to reform. Nonetheless, it seems that the system is still working, the worst case scenario has been avoided and corporate agendas are switching back from survival to value creation again.

The principles described in this book have not changed based on recent events. Valuation is still conducted in the same way and with the same methodology. Richard Branson has been quoted saying that 'it is easy to become a millionaire, all you need to do is invest one billion in an airline'. Destroying value has always been easy. However, the opposite, to create value, which is the primary purpose and aim of all organizational activities, is still a worthy challenge to the best and brightest.

> To measure value is consequently only part science, and the rest is experience, judgement and pure luck

Value creation is scientific and specific only to an extent, the rest of the value is created in a myriad of everyday decisions within the organization. To measure value is consequently only part science, and the rest is experience, judgement and pure luck.

Today's capital markets are more demanding than ever. As a response, corporate investors have come to be more demanding and increasingly focused on the creation of shareholder return and the maximization of

Acknowledgements

No literary work can be attributed solely to the efforts of its authors. This book is certainly no exception, especially as it emanates from a number of theoretical areas and practical frameworks in the field of corporate valuation. A first thanks therefore goes to the many authors and great minds behind the books, articles and publications that are listed under 'Further reading' at the end of the book. Their work has served as the foundation for this book and as a very important input to our own contribution.

We are also much obliged to our publishers at Financial Times Prentice Hall, Chris Cudmore and Martina O'Sullivan, who have shown great skill and talent in motivating and coaching us through this second edition.

We would also like to give our warmest thanks to our mentor Kjell A. Nordström, author of *Funky Business* and management guru. He has been a source of inspiration for our eclectic approach through which we have engaged in theories and knowledge from a large number of areas, including those not directly or obviously linked to corporate valuation.

Furthermore, our long-time friend Maria Dorriots, Head of M&A at Hachette Publishing, deserves a special thanks for her invaluable feedback and comments.

Last but not least, much patience and understanding has been afforded us by our wives, Minéa and Annice, and our friends and family who have provided invaluable support.

For any errors that remain, linguistic as well as logical, we alone are responsible.

Publisher's acknowledgements

We are grateful to the following for permission to reproduce copyright material:

Figure 3.3 from *Valuation*, third edition (McKinsey & Co), © John Wiley & Sons Inc. Reprinted with permission of John Wiley & Sons, Inc.; Figure 7.3 adapted from *Competitive strategy: Techniques for Analyzing Industries and Competitors*, The Free Press (Porter, M.E., 1980). Adapted with the permission of The Free Press, a Division of Simon & Schuster, Inc. Copyright © 1980, 1998 by The Free Press. All rights reserved.

In some instances we have been unable to trace the owners of copyright material, and we would appreciate any information that would enable us to do so.

Student

No matter whether you are an MBA student studying corporate finance and corporate valuation or an experienced manager at an executive education programme touching upon valuation issues, students are always looking for shortcuts. Congratulations! This book is one gigantic shortcut to the area of valuation and therefore we do recommend that you read the entire book. It will, in an easy way, explain all areas of corporate valuation and give you the necessary frameworks to work with. If the exam is tomorrow morning, we recommend that you focus on Chapter 4, 'Company valuation – an overview', and either Chapter 5, 'Ratio-based valuation', or Chapter 6, 'Discounted cash flow valuation', depending on your needs for tomorrow.

Equations

As you will see, we have shown the equations in the book in shaded boxes when we first introduce them. When the equations are used in calculations they do not appear shaded. This is in order to help you distinguish the original equations from the applications of them.

Contact us!

If you have any questions, comments or feedback regarding the contents of this book, please email us at **david@frykman.com** or **j@tolleryd.com**.

Profession

Corporate finance professional

We recommend you read the whole book if you wish to refresh your knowledge and skills. Read Chapter 5, 'Ratio-based valuation', Chapter 6, 'Discounted cash flow valuation', and Chapter 7, 'Underlying analysis and key value drivers', if you only wish to freshen up the most used models. Specifically, 'Checking your assumptions' in Chapter 6 will provide you with a toolbox for verifying that your valuation is reasonable. Finally, in order to understand how the theoretical concepts you work with every day translate into concrete strategies for running a business (or perhaps why you, a corporate finance professional, would be well suited as a chief executive officer (CEO)), read Chapter 9, 'Value-based management'.

Private investor

As a private investor, you might have limited time to spend on your valuations. The fastest way to achieve a decent approximation of a corporate value is normally through multiple valuations. Consequently, read Chapter 5, 'Ratio-based valuation'. Complement this with at least a brief reading of Chapter 6, 'Discounted cash flow valuation', to understand the basic concepts and Chapter 8, 'How to value your company in practice – an example', in order to get an explanation of how to apply the presented concepts.

Manager

Chapters 1–3 will provide you with a good understanding of valuation and why it is important to you. Adding to this the sections of Chapter 4, 'Company valuation – an overview', recommended for the 30-minute reader will enable you also to grasp the basics of the most important valuation methods. For an understanding of how to identify the crucial value-increasing variables in your firm and what drives value in the industry you are in, read Chapter 7, 'Underlying analysis and key value drivers'. In addition, and perhaps most importantly for you as a manager, read Chapter 9, 'Value-based management', for a view on how to manage a business in order to achieve maximum value creation.

Available time

30 minutes

OK, so you are in a rush. In Chapter 4, 'Company valuation – an overview', read sub-sections: Theoretical overview, Discounted cash flow (DCF) model, and Valuation models based on multiples. In addition, for a practical application of the full content of this book, read Chapter 8, 'How to value your company in practice – an example'. Study the figures and boxed text.

One hour

In Chapter 4, 'Company valuation – an overview', read the sections specified for the 30-minute reader. Complement this with either Chapter 5, 'Ratio-based valuation', if you would like to know more about ratio-based valuation or Chapter 6, 'Discounted cash flow valuation', if you are more interested in understanding why corporate value equals future discounted cash flows and how to perform a DCF analysis. Finally, spend a considerable percentage of your available time on Chapter 8, 'How to value your company in practice – an example'. Focus on the figures and boxed text.

Two hours

In Chapter 4, 'Company valuation – an overview', read the sections specified for the 30-minute reader. Complement this with Chapter 5, 'Ratio-based valuation' or Chapter 6, 'Discounted cash flow valuation', and Chapter 7, 'Underlying analysis and key value drivers', where the analysis of the company's business and its key value drivers is presented. Last but certainly not least, in order to grasp both the theory and its practical use, study Chapter 8, 'How to value your company in practice – an example'.

In addition, if you are involved in the running of a business, especially if you are part of the management team, we recommend reading Chapter 9, 'Value-based management'.

Eight hours

Read the entire book. Eight hours should be enough!

should read. We have structured the reading guide according to level of previous knowledge, available time and profession.

Level of previous knowledge of corporate valuation

Little or no knowledge

Our advice here is to read the entire book. The book you are holding in your hand is probably the shortest way to learn about the subject of corporate valuation. Standard textbooks typically explain corporate valuation in 500 pages or more and require a fair amount of financial knowledge as well as a large amount of time. In addition, we recommend that you read this book in the order in which the chapters appear since it is structured so as to ease the reader into the universe of corporate valuation.

Medium knowledge

We recommend you read the following chapters: Chapter 4, 'Company valuation – an overview', for a quick but comprehensive outline of the most important corporate valuation techniques in use today; Chapter 5, 'Ratio-based valuation', for an in-depth coverage of ratio-based valuation; and Chapter 6, 'Discounted cash flow valuation', for a detailed account of the so-called McKinsey version of the discounted cash flow (DCF) model. Furthermore, Chapter 7, 'Underlying analysis and key value drivers', will give valuable insights into the most important elements underlying a corporate valuation, and Chapter 8, 'How to value your company in practice – an example', provides a useful practical exercise in valuing our fictitious example company.

Advanced knowledge

If you have extensive previous knowledge of the subject, this book might largely cover things you are already familiar with and you will probably use it mainly to refresh your knowledge of the topic. Our intention has been to explain corporate valuation as easily as possible and consequently you will not find theoretically complex mathematical proofs in the book. However, apart from being suitable for freshening up corporate valuation issues, we believe that the extensive treatment of ratios in Chapter 5, 'Ratio-based valuation', and the analysis of financial as well as operative key value drivers in Chapter 7, 'Underlying analysis and key value drivers', could be of interest. In addition, Chapter 9, 'Value-based management', can also add a practical dimension to your valuation knowledge. Finally, look at the further reading section at the end of the book.

Preface

What's new about the second edition?

In the years between the first and the second edition, we have continued our work as entrepreneurs and investors in small and medium sized companies. Through that work, we have been involved in the typical daily value creation of those companies as CEOs, board members and investors. Additionally, we have also been involved in a number of corporate valuation situations such as capital raisings, mergers, acquisitions and IPOs, where the valuations have been a most critical task. Based on these experiences and the feedback from readers of the first edition, we have rewritten and updated all chapters throughout the book, and specifically all examples and tables including the in-depth valuation of our example company in Chapter 8. We have, in Chapter 4, complemented the overview of all corporate valuation models with the residual income model and so-called venture valuation to make the overview more complete. Also, after specific demands from readers, we have expanded the chapter on multiples (Chapter 5), both extending the presentation of existing multiples such as the P/E multiple and the P/Book value multiple and adding new multiples such as PEG ratios. Finally, in Chapter 6 on DCF valuation, we have revised and improved the section on target capital structure.

Reading guide

This book has been written for readers who may have varying levels of knowledge on the subject of corporate valuation, varying amounts of time to spend and possibly different purposes for learning about the topic. Even though one of our main goals has been to make this book as short as possible, we do not believe that everyone has the time or indeed the desire to read the entire book. With this in mind, we have included the following reading guide that will enable you to decide which parts of this book you

Contents

PEARSON EDUCATION LIMITED

Edinburgh Gate
Harlow CM20 2JE
Tel: +44 (0)1279 623623
Fax: +44 (0)1279 431059
Website: www.pearsoned.co.uk

First published in Great Britain in 2003
Second edition published 2010

Pearson Education is not responsible for the content of third party internet sites.

ISBN: 978-0-273-72910-5

British Library Cataloguing in Publication Data
A catalogue record for this book is available from the British Library

Library of Congress Cataloging-in-Publication Data
A catalog record for this book is available from the Library of Congress

10 9 8 7 6 5 4 3 2 1
14 13 12 11 10

Typeset in 9pt Stone Serif by 30
Printed and bound by Ashford Colour Press, Gosport

The Financial Times Guide to Corporate Valuation

David Frykman and Jakob Tolleryd

Second edition

Financial Times
Prentice Hall
is an imprint of

Harlow, England • London • New York • Boston • San Francisco • Toronto • Sydney • Singapore • Hong Kong
Tokyo • Seoul • Taipei • New Delhi • Cape Town • Madrid • Mexico City • Amsterdam • Munich • Paris • Milan

Table 2.1: Mobitronics key facts

Founded	1992
Turnover 2009	€4,640 m
EBITDA	44.3%
Revenue growth 2009	11%
Market share	22%
No. of customers	9,130,000
No. of employees	4,550

Currently the company generates approximately €42 per customer/month. Mobitronics has a larger share of corporate customers than its competitors. Since corporate clients are more loyal and engender less risk of default, this has resulted in more stable revenues. The current customer distribution is 65 per cent corporate clients and 35 per cent private. In addition, while pursuing its differentiation strategy, Mobitronics has managed to grow with the market and has defended its market share successfully.

Mobitronics has just begun to see significant economies of scale in its operations. Costs are, as a percentage of revenues, 15 per cent salaries, 12 per cent traffic charges, 7 per cent reseller commissions and 5 per cent in depreciation.

Mobitronics has managed to grow with the market and has defended its market share successfully

The company operates only in Benelux, a market that has grown historically by 15–20 per cent annually, but which is currently growing at the rate of about 10 per cent per annum. For the time being, the company has no business activity outside Benelux or any plans for further internationalization.

Mobitronics has two main competitors. They both employ a strategy of cost leadership and essentially provide the same selection of basic services. They have a customer market share of about 29 per cent and 49 per cent respectively. Mobitronics faces increased competition from the development of new technology. A few companies are about to enter the market with fourth-generation mobile technology as well as Voice Over IP and this will increase competition and potentially create price pressure.

The total value of the Benelux market today is approximately €21,000m annually and analysts expect both the market and Mobitronics to grow at 10–11 per cent per annum over the next five years. Beyond that, technology shifts make forecasts difficult.

In the next chapter we will deal with some different valuation scenarios and we will be using Mobitronics as an example.

3

When do you need to value a company?

What topics are covered in this chapter?

- Raising capital for growth
- Creating an incentive programme to keep and attract employees
- Executing a merger, acquisition or divestiture
- Performing an initial public offering (IPO)
- Summary

Whether you are a prospective investor, a member of the board, or the manager of a company, knowing and understanding the value of your company is always beneficial and, in some situations, essential. Corporate valuations are carried out in a number of different situations, by a number of different parties with a number of different intentions. These are important to understand and recognize. Therefore, we will examine some of these situations below. We will illustrate why a valuation is needed, see who typically performs the valuation and consider what objectives the different parties to the valuation normally have.

> Corporate valuations are carried out in a number of different situations, by a number of different parties with a number of different intentions

We will follow our model company Mobitronics and its journey from the first round of financing in 1994 to its initial public offering (IPO).

In this chapter we will describe the following valuation scenarios:

- Raising capital for growth
- Creating an incentive programme to keep and attract employees
- Executing a merger, acquisition or divestiture
- Conducting an IPO.

Raising capital for growth

Back in early 1994, two years into the existence of Mobitronics, the founders realized that their original finances would not carry the company through the product development, marketing and recruitment required to bring the venture up to speed. As is usual, a lack of capital prevented the company from growing faster and the founders decided to attempt to acquire financing from external investors in order to carry out the expansion.

They calculated the capital requirements until cash flow break-even at €2m. With the help of a friend at a consultancy they wrote a business plan that was presented to a selection of venture capitalists and private investors (sometimes called business angels) in London and Amsterdam. In the end they entered negotiations with three separate suitors. Two of them were venture capital firms that specialized in investments in early-stage companies. The other was a business angel, a private person who invested part of her private fortune in early-stage companies. Despite the fact that one of the venture capital firms offered the most favourable conditions for the €2m investment, the original founders opted for the other venture capital firm and the business angel. Their reasons for this were the industrial competence and superior business networks those investors gave access to, as well as the personal chemistry between the founders and the investor representatives that they would later work with.

In practice, the transaction was executed through exchanging newly issued Mobitronics shares for capital. As the capital was intended for use within the company, a new share issue was carried out. Obviously, an important consideration was how much of the company the external investors should receive for their €2m investment. In this case, the entire company was judged to be worth €4m before the investment. In other words, the so-called post-money valuation was €6m and the pre-money valuation was €4m, as illustrated by the table below (amounts in €m):

Valuation of Mobitronics (pre-money)	4
+ investment	2
= Valuation of Mobitronics (post-money)	6

To calculate the amount of the company's capital stock that would now be owned by the new investors, their investment of €2m was divided into the post-money valuation of €6m.

Percentage of shares owned by investors after capital injection =

Investment in euros/post-money valuation

$$\frac{€2m}{€6m} = 0.33 = 33\%$$

Hence, a €6m valuation of Mobitronics gave the investors 33 per cent of the capital collectively.

If instead the pre-money valuation had been only €2m, the calculation would have been the following:

$$\frac{€2m}{€4m} = 0.5 = 50\%$$

Accordingly, the difference between a valuation of €4m and €6m meant the difference between 33 per cent and 50 per cent of the total number of shares to the investors. By contrast, if the pre-money valuation had been €6m then the situation would have been:

$$\frac{€2m}{€8m} = 0.25 = 25\%$$

The investors would then be left with only 25 per cent of the outstanding shares in the company. In summary, the different scenarios give the following results (amounts in €m):

Pre-money valuation	Capital injection	Post-money valuation	Investor ownership
2	2	4	50%
4	2	6	33%
6	2	8	25%

So, the valuation of the company is important to both the current owners and the incoming owners. While this type of deal is normally carried out in good spirit (since the entrepreneur(s) and the investor(s) will work together after the deal is closed), existing owners benefit from a high valuation of the company and the prospective investors profit from a low one.

In an early stage investment there are typically two main parties who value the company: the entrepreneur(s) (together with other early owners) and the investor(s), for example, a venture capitalist or business angel.

A company seeking venture capital is often not profitable, nor cash flow positive, and the forecasts for when positive earnings or cash flow can be expected are fairly unreliable.

> Valuation of companies in early stages is greatly dependent on the negotiation skills of the parties

How the focus in valuation shifts during the different stages of a company's development can be illustrated as in Figure 3.1.

A combination of the valuation models presented later in this book could and should be used to get as many different reference points as possible.

However, more than anything else the process of determining company value in these early stages depends on the credibility and the track record

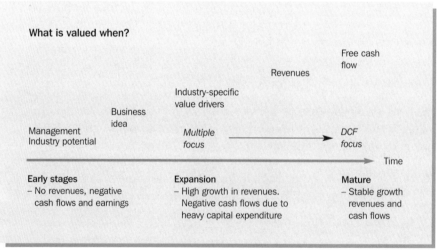

What is valued when?

Free cash flow

Revenues

Industry-specific value drivers

Business idea

Management
Industry potential

Multiple focus —————▶ *DCF focus*

Time

Early stages
– No revenues, negative cash flows and earnings

Expansion
– High growth in revenues. Negative cash flows due to heavy capital expenditure

Mature
– Stable growth revenues and cash flows

FIGURE 3.1   What is valued when: business idea and management at early stages, industry value driver (e.g. clients) and revenues for growth and expansion, cash flow when mature

of the management team, the industry opportunity and, importantly, the negotiation skills of the parties. As long as the amounts raised are fairly small and the transactions not very complex, then the actual valuation and related negotiations will be carried out by the parties involved without outside help from advisors such as investment banks.

Points to consider when raising venture capital are as follows:

■ How much of the company is for sale? If the current owners wish to remain in control by force of ownership, they must control more than 50 per cent (of the votes), and other instruments such as shareholder agreements or preferential shares should not be allowed to limit their influence unduly.

■ The mandatory business plan, which all potential investors will require and scrutinize before investing, is the main sales tool in the process. Note that overselling in the business plan could be a costly way to increase short-term valuation as the business plan is to be considered a mutually agreed plan for the future between the current owners and the venture capitalist. Major negative deviations are not generally well-received and it is not uncommon to tie follow-up investments to performance according to the business plan or in fact adjust the valuation in hindsight.

■ What skills and network does the company require? What does the investor offer and how does this fit with the company's needs? For example, if there are plans for expansion, where will this expansion take place? If it is outside the company's home market, it may be better to approach international venture capital that can also bring you knowledge and networks in the markets the company is about to enter.

There are different types of capital. A main distinction is whether the company needs intelligent capital that offers operational know-how and strategic advantages or financial capital that perhaps does not add as much know-how. Venture capitalists, industrial capitalists and business angels typically fall under the first category whereas some institutional capital falls under the second.

■ Intelligent capital – adds know-how and strategic advantages

■ Financial capital – cash only

Creating an incentive programme to keep and attract employees

When Mobitronics had been in operation for approximately four years the company had 150 employees. A frequent problem was keeping the most competent personnel and attracting new talent. One alternative was to increase salaries significantly, but as pay was already one of the main costs, incentives that did not increase fixed costs or further strained the company's liquidity were preferred.

Mobitronics' management decided to construct an incentive programme with shareholder-like effects for the employees. The benefit of such a programme is its limited effect on company cash flow and the alignment of shareholder and employee objectives and goals to maximize value creation. The negative aspects of such a programme are, among other things, that it might be fairly complicated and include a number of hours with expensive lawyers. Also, the incentive is affected by many factors that are not under the control of the employees – interest rates, general market sentiment, etc. Finally, in order for employees to be able to realize their potential gains from the programme, it must be possible to sell or in some other way cash in on the investment: otherwise, employees could be locked into the investment for longer than they wish. Generally, incentive programmes with shareholder-like effects are most common and make most sense in companies with traded shares or with a clear path towards a stock-market listing or trade sale.

There are a number of ways of structuring such an incentive programme. The most common types of incentive programme with shareholder-like effects are:

- A directed new share issue to all or some of the employees.
- A convertible bond issue. Basically, the employees lend money to the company against interest on a convertible bond. At a designated date or during a designated period, the employees have the right (but not the obligation) to convert their bond investment into a certain number of shares at a pre-determined price. If an employee does not wish to convert the bond into shares, the company is obliged to repay the loan with interest to the employee. (Theoretically, a convertible bond is a standard interest rate bond plus a call option on the company's shares.)
- A stock option issue, sometimes called warrants. The employees purchase the right (but not the obligation) to buy a certain number of shares in the company on a certain date (exercise date) or during a certain period

(exercise period) in the future at a pre-determined price (the exercise price). For this right, the employees pay a premium, which is calculated using the so-called Black and Scholes formula.[1]

■ In some countries, so-called employee options programmes are possible. The company itself can then generally determine the premium the employees have to pay for the option to acquire shares in the future. In such programmes, usually the premium is set to zero and options are in fact given to the employee. In return, the options are tied to employment and when the employee leaves the employment, the options are forfeited.

Mobitronics' management decided against a share issue, since it would have meant that the company would have had a large number of shareholders, something that would increase the complexity and bureaucracy in major decisions. The company also decided against an employee options programme since it would have unfavourable tax consequences both for the company and for the employees. The choice then lay between a convertible bond issue and a stock options issue. We will not cover the advantages and disadvantages of these two types of incentive programmes in depth here. What is important is that they both necessitate a valuation of the company. For the convertible bond issue you need to know the future conversion price of the stock (and hence the value of the company since value per stock equals company market value/number of shares). In addition, a valuation today is needed when issuing the convertibles as a yardstick for setting the conversion price. For the stock options issue, one of the input variables in the Black and Scholes formula is the current price per share of the company in question (again calculated as the company's market value divided by the amount of shares in the company).

Options and convertible bond programmes both necessitate a valuation of the company

It may seem strange and perhaps even unnecessary to value the company when the management usually wants to offer shareholder-like incentives for the employees at an advantageous price. It could instead appear reasonable that the current owners agree on a valuation low enough to ensure that employees are given an attractive offer. However, in many countries, the valuation of the company must be based on a market value for tax reasons. If not, tax authorities can claim that the

[1] The Black and Scholes formula was first presented in 1973 in the article 'The pricing of options and corporate liabilities' by Fisher Black and Myron Scholes. It has since then been used widely when calculating the theoretical value of an option. For more about options, see the Further reading section at the end of this book.

incentive programme is to be treated as salaried income for the employees. The consequence is that an employee is obliged to pay income tax and the company to pay social security expenses on the entire programme. A common stipulation from tax authorities is that the price of the share, convertible or option, which employees are entitled to acquire, must reflect a market-based value.

When dealing with tax authorities, and this is likely to be universal, it is better to be safe than sorry and have an independent party, often an accountancy firm or an investment bank, to do the valuation in order to be able to argue effectively for the objectivity of the valuation used.

Figure 3.2 shows a generic theoretical development of a company's value and cash flow.

Executing a merger, acquisition or divestiture

When Mobitronics had been in business for ten years the company was contacted by representatives from PayMobile, a small niche player with a strong competence in internet-based, mobile applications. The representatives for PayMobile expressed an interest in selling the company. After thoroughly analyzing the acquisition opportunity, Mobitronics' management believed there was a clear strategic fit between the companies and that an acquisition of PayMobile would strengthen Mobitronics' service

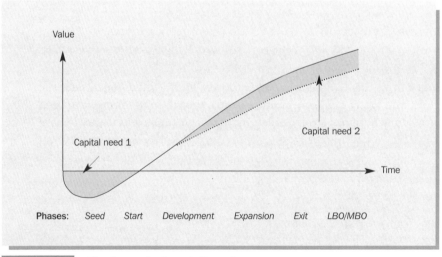

FIGURE 3.2   The 'expected' evolution of a company

offering and R&D competence. However, as cash reserves were limited, Mobitronics would carry out the acquisition only if PayMobile would accept Mobitronics' stocks as payment.

In a share-for-share transaction both the acquisition target and the acquirer need to be valued. In this situation both sides will want to maximize the value of their respective asset and minimize the value of the other – all in order to achieve the maximum relative value. Normally, a mixture of valuation models is used to get a number of reference points for the valuation discussion. Typically, some type of standalone DCF valuation is used for a fundamental discussion of the two companies, their operations and their future earnings potential. In addition, financial and operative ratios are used to allow for effective comparisons in the discussions and negotiations.

The idea behind this kind of transaction in valuation terms is that the value of the combined entity will be more than that of the separate entities. In industrial transactions, the price that the acquirer is willing to pay usually exceeds (and, in theory, should always exceed) the value a financial buyer would ascribe to the company. This is because the industrial party can pay not only for the pure financial value, but also for synergies and other operating and strategic values. These are values the financial buyer or the capital market simply cannot realize. Since an industrial acquirer normally can pay a higher price than the financial markets, price

> Private equity firms have been using a much higher leverage than industrial acquirers and therefore have been able to pay higher prices

is normally not the only critical concern. Instead, the loss of independence and management issues are often of equal importance (sometimes to shareholders' despair). However, as has been seen in transactions in the past decade, it is not uncommon that financial buyers, typically private equity firms, have a much more aggressive view of how much debt the acquisition target can bear. In other words, private equity firms have been using a much higher leverage than industrial acquirers and therefore have been able to pay higher prices. (We will go through the mechanism of why higher leverage results in higher valuations in Chapter 6.)

When valuation is conducted in an industrial deal the valuation technique differs slightly from earlier situations discussed in this chapter. This is because the synergies, economies of scale and other strategic assets have a value that needs to be added to the value of the target company (see Figure 3.3).

Thus, when Mobitronics was evaluating the option to acquire PayMobile, the valuation steps were the following (see Figure 3.4):

■ Financial value of PayMobile according to a DCF valuation and various ratios: €1m.

■ Potential value with internal operating and strategic synergies: €1.2m.

■ Potential value with internal operating and strategic improvements and with external operating and strategic opportunities such as divestitures, acquisitions, etc.: €1.3m.

■ Optimal value adding financial re-engineering such as streamlining the capital structure and debt portfolio: €1.35m.

As we can see, even though the financial value of PayMobile was approximated to be around €1m at the time, Mobitronics, being an industrial acquirer, could be willing to pay a significant premium on top of that. Just how much more is usually decided through negotiations. The acquirer will of course be willing to pay more if the realization of the synergies and other value-creating efforts are deemed to be easy and of low risk. Since it is the acquirer who will be in charge of realizing the synergies and there-

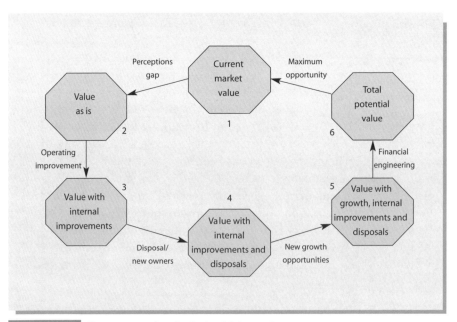

FIGURE 3.3   Company value for industrial enquirer

Source: *Valuation*, 3rd edition, McKinsey & Co.

fore who bears the risk, their full value is rarely paid, and theoretically should never be paid, to the current owners of the acquisition target. But the important point is that the existence of industrial and strategic synergies creates value for the industrial party but not for financial buyers.

Not surprisingly, the representatives from PayMobile initially argued for a valuation far greater than Mobitronics was willing to pay. After some negotiations, the parties agreed that the PayMobile owners would get one-twelfth, or 8.3 per cent, of the outstanding shares in Mobitronics after the transaction in exchange for 100 per cent of the shares in PayMobile.

When valuing companies in an industrial transaction, the need for advisors is really dependent on the size of the transaction, i.e. the size of the respective companies. Smaller companies usually conduct their own valuations, the slightly larger perhaps get help from an accounting firm or an independent consultant, while large companies acquire advice from investment banks. The purchasing company has to have an active role in the process as all synergies and strategic values have to be measured and priced correctly.

> Smaller companies usually conduct their own valuations

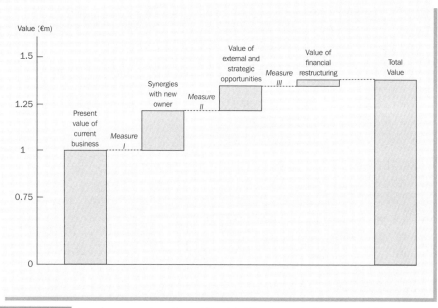

FIGURE 3.4 The increase in value of PayMobile through the eyes of Mobitronics

Performing an initial public offering (IPO)

After five years of further operations, the management of Mobitronics decided to pursue a stock market listing. The reasons for this were:

■ To raise capital for further expansion.

■ To ensure easy access to financial markets if and when new capital was needed for further investments.

■ As a way to receive media coverage and make the brand and the company more well-known in order to attract prospective customers and employees.

■ To get a price for the company's shares in order to facilitate further acquisitions as well as employee incentive programmes.

The preparations for a stock market listing are substantial and much management time has to be devoted to the process. The process and its constituent parts can be described as shown in Figure 3.5.

One part of this preparation process is the pricing of the shares to be introduced on the exchange, which, naturally, is based on a valuation of the entire company. As the shares are to be marketed to investors, private individuals and institutions with limited knowledge of the company, it is crucial that an investment bank with a good reputation can guarantee the quality of the valuation. This is essential to raise interest in the stock and to encourage investors to trust their funds with the company.

Furthermore, an investment bank will add valuable insights as to current investor sentiment and how the market is likely to price the stock (and hence the company) once it is traded. An important aspect concerning the valuation for an IPO is the 'equity story', i.e. the positioning of the company stock relative to the market.

Before the pricing of the shares in the IPO, the owners or the board of directors of the company and the investment bank negotiate the valuation. This is because the owners generally want a higher valuation and the investment bank, which is to market and sell the shares to its private and institutional customers, wants a lower valuation. It is customary to sell shares at an IPO at a discount to the perceived actual value and it is therefore not unusual to see shares soaring on their first day of trading. The level of discount varies depending on general market conditions, type of company, etc. but is usually in the range of 15–30 per cent on the equity value.

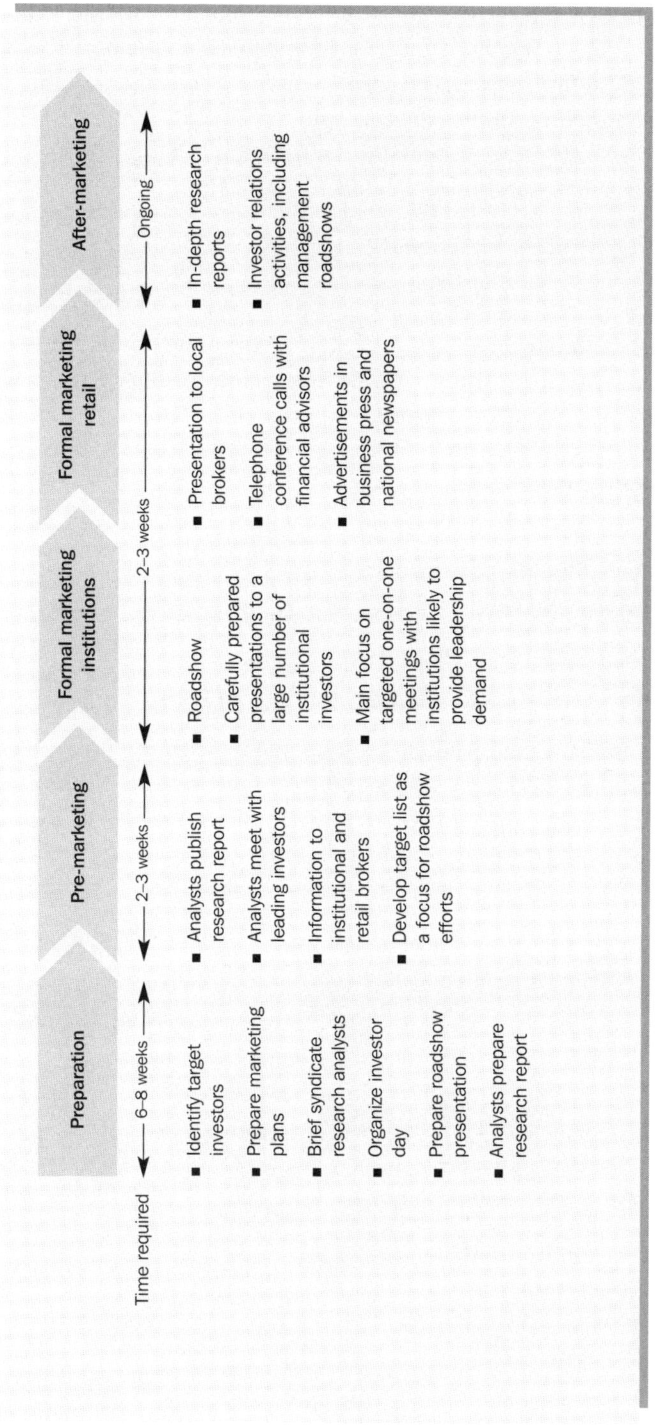

Preparation	Pre-marketing	Formal marketing institutions	Formal marketing retail	After-marketing
Time required → 6–8 weeks →	→ 2–3 weeks →	→ 2–3 weeks →		→ Ongoing →
■ Identify target investors ■ Prepare marketing plans ■ Brief syndicate research analysts ■ Organize investor day ■ Prepare roadshow presentation ■ Analysts prepare research report	■ Analysts publish research report ■ Analysts meet with leading investors ■ Information to institutional and retail brokers ■ Develop target list as a focus for roadshow efforts	■ Roadshow ■ Carefully prepared presentations to a large number of institutional investors ■ Main focus on targeted one-on-one meetings with institutions likely to provide leadership demand	■ Presentation to local brokers ■ Telephone conference calls with financial advisors ■ Advertisements in business press and national newspapers	■ In-depth research reports ■ Investor relations activities, including management roadshows

FIGURE 3.5 The IPO process

In the IPO, the shares of Mobitronics were priced at €5 per share. With 10 million shares, this meant a company valuation of €50m. The board of directors of Mobitronics argued for a higher price but the investment bank emphasized the importance of successful trading in the stock after the IPO (i.e. a rising share price). Soon after the flotation of Mobitronics' stock, the stock price rose to €6, valuing Mobitronics at €60m.

Summary

There are a number of situations when a corporate valuation is needed, which can arise from the very early phases of development to the very late. Certainly, not all companies experience the same type of development, but usually a growth company encounters one or several of the situations described. In this chapter we dealt with the following valuation scenarios:

- Raising capital for growth and the choice of potential investors.
- Stock-based incentive programmes to keep and attract talent.
- Mergers, acquisitions and divestitures.
- A listing of the company's shares through an IPO.

Generally, in a valuation, there are two parties with opposite objectives – one wants to maximize valuation and the other wants to minimize it. The seller (the company, the entrepreneurs, the owners) as well as the acquirer/ investor generally have advisors in the form of investment banks (in larger transactions), accounting firms or consultants (smaller transactions).

In the next chapter we will present an overview of the most used corporate valuation methods.

4

Company valuation – an overview

What topics are covered in this chapter?

- Theoretical overview
- The most important valuation models
- What models to use?
- Summary

Many different models and methods exist for valuing a company. Some are used only in specific situations, some are more or less always part of a valuation exercise, and others are used mainly in conjunction with other models. This chapter is not a comprehensive presentation of all existing valuation models, but rather a brief overview of the most important ones. In the coming chapters, we will describe in more detail the two most commonly used: the discounted cash flow (DCF model) and multiple valuation.

In this particular chapter we will be outlining the following:

- A theoretical overview of various valuation techniques
- Descriptions of models for valuation
- Recommendations for which models to use.

Before moving on, it is important to point out that 'value' varies from being a range to a very specific number. Many people expect the value to always be an exact number whereas this is often only true in specific situations. When doing a valuation, the value may be a range with rather non-academic variations depending on what model you use or what assumptions you make. On the other hand, at a certain point in time and in a particular situation, the valuation of a company may instead be a very exact number. For example, when Microsoft was planning to make a public tender for Yahoo in 2008, the valuation was most likely a range at the beginning of the process. At the day of going public with the bid, however, the valuation had been narrowed down to exactly $31 per share or $44.6 bn for all the outstanding shares.

In addition, when contemplating the value of a company, remember the number one rule of finance: *the value of an asset is what someone else is willing to pay for it.* If you are a seller, this rule holds no matter what the theory or your personal feeling says. Parameters

The value of an asset is what someone else is willing to pay for it

such as liquidity, the buyers' access to capital, etc. very much determine the price. You may own an umbrella in platinum but it will not render a high price in the desert. At that point, the value might be higher to you than to the buyer and you are, indirectly, the one willing to pay the highest price by not selling your asset.

Kjell A. Nordström, well-known author, professor and mentor of the authors of this book, often says 'better roughly right than exactly wrong'; an idiom that very much holds true in the field of valuation. You may use a theoretically correct model and be very detailed and diligent in its use but by making one wrong assumption you get the value absolutely wrong. The number you have calculated may, of course, be theoretically correct but practically off target. It is this basic fact of valuation that makes it so intriguing – it takes a combination of science and art.

This book only covers valuation models that analyze the actual company, rather than those that focus on the movements of its shares in capital markets, which is usually referred to as technical analysis. Moreover, all the valuation models presented below assume that

The two most common approaches to valuation are the McKinsey DCF model and ratio-based valuation

the company is a 'going concern', which means that the company is assumed to continue with its activities and not be wound down or broken up. Such circumstances call for specific valuation models that are outside the scope of this book. Furthermore, we will not describe valuation of financial instruments, such as options, futures or insurances. We direct the interested reader to a list of specialist literature found in the Further reading section at the end of this book. Also outside the scope of this book are specific valuation models that are adapted to certain industry sectors and for companies in developing countries, where valuations need to account for factors such as political risk or extremely high inflation. Here again, we draw attention to specialist literature. That said, the information provided in this book is a good platform for most valuation situations – the fundamental logic is the same even though the method might differ.

Theoretical overview

There are a few important concepts that need to be explained before moving on to the specific valuation models: the difference between equity and enterprise value, the difference between fundamental and relative valuation, and the difference in basing the valuation on cash flow, returns or operating variables.

Equity value vs enterprise value

An important distinction is between equity value and enterprise value:

■ **Equity value** The equity value of an enterprise is equal to the value of the shareholders' claims in the company. Equity value is sometimes called market value (MV) since it expresses the accumulated market value of all the company shares. It is important to distinguish between the accounted equity in the balance sheet and the market value of equity. To arrive at a value per share, divide the value of the company's equity by the total number of shares outstanding. If the company is publicly traded, the value of the equity equals the market capitalization of the company (given that you agree with the market valuation of the company).

■ **Enterprise value** The enterprise value, on the other hand, is the value of the entire company, the value to all claimholders in the company. The enterprise value consists of the market value of the company's equity plus the market value of the company's debt, its pension provisions, minority interests and other claims. The relationship between equity and enterprise value can be explained graphically as shown in Figure 4.1.

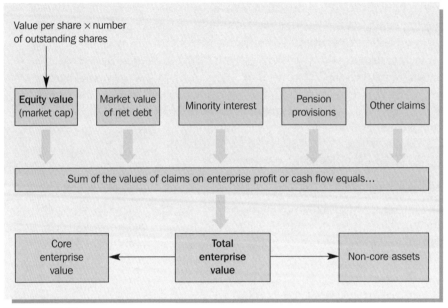

Value per share × number of outstanding shares

| Equity value (market cap) | Market value of net debt | Minority interest | Pension provisions | Other claims |

Sum of the values of claims on enterprise profit or cash flow equals...

| Core enterprise value | ← | Total enterprise value | → | Non-core assets |

FIGURE 4.1 Relationship between equity and enterprise value

Enterprise value = equity value + market value of net debt + minority interests + pension provisions + other claims.

Equity value = enterprise value − market value of net debt − minority interests − pension provisions − other claims.

Value per share = value of equity (for quoted stocks equal to market capitalization)/number of shares.

Fundamental vs relative valuation

There are two different ways to approach a valuation: fundamental or relative. Fundamental valuations are, as can be deduced from the name, calculated based on company fundamentals. These methods produce an explicit value of the company based on certain fundamental economic information that is relevant to the company and its future. This type of valuation is also referred to as a standalone valuation. Relative valuations (i.e. relative multiples), by contrast, apply a relation of a specific financial or operational characteristic from a similar company or the industry to the company being valued. In other words, relative valuations express the value of the company as a multiple of a specific statistic like sales or earnings.

Relative valuations express the value of the company as a multiple of a specific statistic like sales or earnings

Relative valuation has an inherent danger that is worth mentioning. If the companies that you use as a base for the relative valuation are incorrectly valued, you will apply the same error when using the multiple on your own company. Remember, for example, the valuations of internet companies in the late 1990s and how using the multiples of the time produced values that were not possible to defend fundamentally.

Basis for valuations – cash flow, returns, assets or operational variables

When calculating the enterprise or equity value and when conducting a fundamental or relative valuation, different bases can be used. For example, in a cash flow model, the basis of the valuation is either the cash flow to equity investors (dividends) or to both equity and debt holders (free cash flow). In a return-based model, the valuation is based instead on the company's capital stock, and the difference between the return on the capital stock and the cost of capital. In an asset-based model, the basis is instead an asset within the company, typically the net asset value. Finally, in some cases operational variables such as number of subscribers or production capacity are used.

An overview of the corporate valuation models could look like that shown in Figure 4.2.

| | | **Valuation basis** | | |
		Cash flow	Returns/earnings	Assets
Valuation approach	Fundamental	DCF, CFROI, Real options, DDM	EVA, Residual income	NAV
	Relative	EV/EBITDA, EV/EBIT, EV/FCF	P/E, PEG	P/B

FIGURE 4.2 Overview of the corporate valuation models

The most important fundamental valuation models

On the following pages, we will describe a number of different models. Some can be used in many situations and others only in specific ones.

Valuation models based on cash flow

Discounted cash flow (DCF) model

In the discounted cash flow (DCF) model, you calculate the enterprise value by estimating all future free cash flow streams and discount them back to today using the appropriate cost of capital. Usually the weighted average cost of capital (WACC) is used, which weighs the cost of equity with the cost of debt. The DCF model is divided into two parts. The first part, often called the explicit period, is where free cash flow and WACC are forecasted explicitly for every year and the cash streams are discounted back to today. The second part, often called the terminal value period, is where the cost of capital and the growth rate are assumed to be constant and the present value of all cash streams from the first year after the explicit period to infinity is calculated. The formula for the DCF model looks like this:

The discounted cash flow (DCF) model = the enterprise value to all future cash flows discounted back to today using the appropriate cost of capital.

$$EV = \frac{FCF_1}{(1 + WACC)} + \frac{FCF_2}{(1 + WACC)^2} + \ldots + \frac{FCF_n}{(1 + WACC)^n} + \frac{TV}{(1 + WACC)^n}$$

where

$$TV = \frac{FCF_{n+1}}{(WACC - g)}$$

where EV is the enterprise value, FCF is future free cash flows in a certain year, WACC is the weighted average cost of capital, TV is the terminal value, g is the growth rate of the free cash flow after year n and n is number of years in the explicit period.

Since the so-called McKinsey version of the DCF model is the most used valuation model for a number of good reasons, we will describe this model in detail in Chapter 6.

Cash flow return on investment (CFROI)

Instead of computing the value of the enterprise as the present value of all future free cash flows, as in the DCF model, one can instead calculate a return ratio that expresses the company's current or future ability to produce free cash flow. A popular method for this is known as cash flow return on investment (CFROI). Originally designed by the Holt Value Consultants, CFROI can be defined as the sustainable cash flow a business generates in a given year as a percentage of the cash invested in the company's assets. You can think of CFROI as a weighted average internal rate of return (IRR) of all the projects within the company. Usually, it is expressed as:

$$\text{Gross cash investment} = \frac{CF_1}{(1+CFROI)} + \frac{CF_2}{(1+CFROI^2)} + \ldots + \frac{CF_n}{(1+CFROI)^n} + \frac{TV}{(1+CFROI)^n}$$

where gross cash investment is the total inflation-adjusted gross cash investment made by all lenders and investors, CF is the inflation-adjusted annual cash flow, TV is the inflation-adjusted terminal value of all future cash flows from year n to infinity, and n is the average economic life of the firm's assets.

The calculated CFROI can be compared with the firm's current or real (inflation-adjusted) historical cost of capital or against real industry rate of returns.

Dividend discount model (DDM)

The dividend discount model (DDM) is not a cash flow-based model in the traditional sense. Instead, according to DDM, the equity value equals all future cash flows in the form of dividends to shareholders discounted back to today. In other words, the model suggests forecasting all future company dividends and discounting them back to today to receive the value of the company's equity. There are two distinct parts to the calculation. Firstly, dividends are forecasted for each and every year, typically the first five to 10 years, and then discounted back to today using the appropriate cost of capital. Secondly, after the explicit period, long-term dividend growth and the appropriate long-term cost of capital need to be forecasted in

The dividend discount model (DDM) equals the equity value to the value of all future dividends discounted back to today using the appropriate cost of capital

order to determine the so-called terminal value, the value of all financial flows after the explicit period to infinity. The terminal value then needs to be discounted back to the present. The cost of capital used in each calculation should reflect the inherent risk in that particular cash flow. The higher the risk, the higher the cost of capital.

Note that only one cost of capital and one growth rate are used in the terminal value calculation. This means in turn that it is necessary to assume a constant growth rate and cost of capital after the explicit period. Or, expressed differently, the explicit period must be extended so that it covers all years where a constant growth rate and/or cost of capital cannot be assumed. The formula can be expressed as:

$$MV = \frac{D_1}{(1+k)} + \frac{D_2}{(1+k^2)} + \dots + \frac{D_n}{(1+k^n)} + \frac{TV}{(1+k)^n}$$

where

$$TV = \frac{D_{n+1}}{C_E - g}$$

where MV is the market value of equity, D is the dividend in a certain year, k is the cost of capital, C_E is the cost of equity, g is the constant growth rate of the dividends after year n, TV is the terminal value and n is the number of years in the explicit period.

Real options valuation

Since the publication of Fisher Black and Myron Scholes' ground-breaking article 'The pricing of options and corporate liabilities' in 1973, option valuation has been used frequently by investors, traders and others to calculate the theoretical value of stock options, interest rate options, and all other kinds of options traded all over the world. The idea behind the pricing of options is to determine the correct theoretical price of the option in order to ascertain whether a certain option is over- or under-valued in the marketplace. It is only in the last few years that option valuation has been recognized as an alternative to standard net present value calculations in the valuation of investment opportunities in real markets and as a company or project valuation tool.

A financial option gives its owner the right to buy (call option) or sell (put option) a certain specified underlying asset (a stock, bond, amount of gold, etc.) at a specified price (the exercise price) within a certain period of time (the exercise period), but with no obligation to do so. For this right the owner pays a premium (the price of the option).

The idea behind real options is similar to the idea of financial options. Consider for example a company that has identified an opportunity (an option), a project with a certain required investment today and a certain additional investment in six months' time (the exercise price). In six months' time, if the opportunity looks promising, i.e. the expected net present value of the project is higher than the exercise price (the investment) of the option, the option is exercised and the project goes ahead. If the project does not look promising, i.e. the net present value of the project is lower than the exercise price (the investment) of the option, the option is not used and the only loss is the price of the option paid, the premium. The point of real options valuation is that it takes into consideration the flexibility that is inherent in many projects (or in entire companies) in a way that a DCF valuation does not. With real options, management possibilities to expand an investment or to abandon a project are given a correct value. Or, stated differently, real option valuation might produce positive net present values where standard net present value calculations produce negative ones. This is because the flexibility of the project or the investment is given a value.

> Real options valuation is a powerful tool in investment-intensive industries where companies make investments in sequences involving a high degree of uncertainty

Certainly, real options valuation brings more to the table in some industries than in others. Specifically, real options valuation is a powerful tool in investment-intensive industries where companies make investments in sequences involving a high degree of uncertainty. A small investment today that gives the opportunity to either continue with a larger investment later or abandon the project altogether is much like a stock option where a small premium is paid today in order to have the opportunity, but not the obligation, to buy the stock later. Examples of such industries include energy (particularly oil and gas), all R&D-intensive industries such as biotechnology, pharmaceutical and high-tech, as well as industries with high marketing investments.

Recently, a number of financial authorities have argued that real options valuation is a valuable tool for the valuation of almost any type of company. The idea is that all unexplored avenues for future cash flow, for example possible new products, new segments or new markets, could or even would be best valued through real options valuation. They want to divide the valuation of a company in the following manner:

Enterprise value = value of existing operations (= value of all discounted future cash flows from present projects)

+ value of the company portfolio of real options (= value of future potential projects)

The value of existing operations is calculated by using one of the valuation models mentioned in this chapter, for example the DCF model. Since we lift the value of future potential operations out of the calculation, the projections for future free cash flow are easier to perform. Thereafter, the value of the company's various other business opportunities in its industry or in adjacent industries is calculated using real options valuation. The two values are then simply added together to give the total enterprise value.

Generally, real options are more a conceptual way of thinking about projects, investments and company opportunities than a practical valuation technique. When used in practice, the value of real options is calculated using the Black and Scholes valuation model for valuing financial options. The Black and Scholes model requires a number of variables in order to calculate the value of the option. When calculating the value of real options, these variables are represented by the fundamental variables of the project, investment or company in question. Since calculations of option values quickly become rather mathematically complex, we refer the interested reader to the literature specified in the Further reading section at the end of this book.

Valuation models based on returns

Residual income model

The term residual income (sometimes called economic profit) refers to the real profit a company produces in contrast to the accounting profit as decided by accounting principles. Residual income takes into consideration not only the company's cost of debt but also the company's cost for equity financing, i.e. the opportunity cost of capital for equity investors.

This has the important implication that a company must not only break even but also make a profit large enough to justify the cost of capital it is using. Residual income can mathematically be expressed as:

$$RI = (R_E - C_E) \times BV_t$$

where RI is the residual income, R_E is the return on equity, C_E is the cost of equity and BV is the book value of the equity at the beginning of the year t.

A residual income model values a company by using a combination of the company's book value and a present value of the company's future residual income. It can be expressed as:

$$\text{Enterprise value} = BV + (RI/(1 + C_E)^1 + RI/(1+C_E)^2 + \ldots RI/(1+C_E)^t + TV/(1 + C_E)^t$$

where BV is the current book value of equity for the company and RI is the future residual income, i.e. the amounts by which profits are expected to exceed the required rate of return on equity, C_E is the cost of equity and t is the number of years in the explicit period.

And where TV is calculated as:

$$TV = BV_t \times RI_t/(C_E - g)$$

where BV_t is the book value at time t, RI_t is the residual income in year t, C_E is the required rate of return on equity and g is the constant growth rate from year t to infinity.

Unlike models that discount dividends or cash flow, in which usually a significant portion of the estimated value comes from its so-called terminal value far away in the future, a residual income model usually derives most of its value from years in the not too distant future. This is because of its reliance on book value, which obviously can be taken directly from the balance sheet. In fact, in many cases the terminal value can be deemed to be zero since the additional value represents such a small portion of the total value. This is a significant advantage over the DCF model since forecasting and estimating errors tend to magnify over time and forecasting 10–15 years into the future can hardly be anything else than an educated guess.

Another advantage is that the residual income model is entirely based on accounting standards with numbers easily available. However, the main disadvantage of the residual income model is that being based on accounting standards, it often fails to reflect the true economic value of assets and cash flows.

Economic value added (EVA)[1]

A slightly altered approach of the residual income model is the so-called economic value added approach, popularly called EVA, which was developed by the consultancy Stern, Stewart & Co. According to this approach, the enterprise value equals the current capital stock plus the value of all future EVA, discounted to the present. The EVA for a given year is the excess return the company enjoys, once all operating as well as capital costs are covered. It is calculated as the difference between the return on capital and the cost of capital, multiplied by the capital stock at the beginning of the year. In other words, in order for the enterprise value to be larger than invested capital, return on invested capital (ROIC) has to exceed the cost of capital over time (Figure 4.3). In order for the enterprise value to be larger than invested capital, ROIC has to exceed the cost of capital over time.

> The EVA for a given year is the excess return the company enjoys, once all operating as well as capital costs are covered

EVA is a fine-tuned variant of residual income or economic profit where a number of adjustments transform financial statement items into statistics suitable for valuation. Specifically, NOPAT (net operating profit after taxes) and the capital stock at the beginning of the year need adjustment. Generally, the adjustments fall into any of the following categories:

- Conversions from financial to cash accounting.
- Conversions from a liquidating perspective to a going-concern perspective.
- Removal of unusual losses or gains.

Economic value added for one year is expressed as:

$$EVA = NOPAT - (WACC \times K)$$

---

[1] Economic value added (EVA) is a registered trademark of Stern, Stewart & Co.

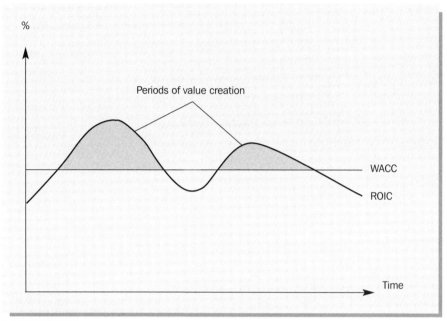

FIGURE 4.3   Relationship between cost of capital, ROIC and value creation

where EVA is economic value added, NOPAT is net operating profit after taxes, but before financing costs and non-cash book-keeping entries (except depreciation), WACC is weighted average cost of capital and K is the capital stock at the beginning of the year, i.e. the sum of all the firm's financing apart from non-interest-bearing liabilities such as accounts payable, accrued wages and accrued taxes.

Alternatively, EVA is expressed as:

$$EVA = (ROIC - WACC) \times K$$

where

$$ROIC = \frac{NOPAT}{K}$$

where EVA is economic value added for year one, ROIC is the return on invested capital for year one, WACC is the weighted average cost of capital, K is the capital stock in the company at the beginning of year one and NOPAT is net operating profit after taxes for year one.

In order for the enterprise value to be larger than invested capital, ROIC has to exceed the cost of capital over time

The result of these calculations states whether the company has a positive or a negative EVA, in other words whether the company is creating or destroying value. In accordance with EVA (and as seen from the formula), a company can only create value in the following ways:

- Increase ROIC and hold WACC and invested capital constant.
- Decrease WACC and hold ROIC and invested capital constant.
- Increase the invested capital in projects/activities yielding a ROIC greater than WACC.
- Withdraw capital from projects/activities that yield a ROIC lower than WACC.
- Create longer periods where the company is expected to earn a ROIC greater than WACC.

However, the goal of the management and board of a company is not to maximize the EVA of one single year but to maximize enterprise value, where enterprise value equals the present value of all future EVA plus the capital stock invested in the company. The aggregated future EVA is generally called market value added (MVA). For publicly traded companies, this can be seen as the difference between a company's market value and the total invested capital in the company. Or expressed differently, the MVA is the market's expectations of future EVAs. When calculating enterprise value, the formula is:

$$EV = K_0 + \frac{EVA_1}{(1 + WACC)^1} + \frac{EVA_2}{(1 + WACC)^2} + \dots + \frac{EVA_n}{(1 + WACC)^n} + \frac{TV}{(1 + WACC)^n}$$

where

$$TV = K_n^* + (ROIC_n - WACC) \times K_n^* \frac{1}{WACC - g}$$

where EV is enterprise value, EVA is economic value added, K is the capital stock in the company, WACC is the weighted average cost of capital, TV is terminal value, ROIC is return on invested capital, K* is the equilibrium value of the capital stock in the terminal year, n is the number of years that the company can enjoy a return on invested capital greater than its cost of capital, and g is the growth rate of future EVA from year n to infinity.

Even though the model might appear completely different from the DCF model, both models will generate the same result if the input data are consistent. And, in fact, it can be shown that:

Enterprise value = present value of future cash flows

= invested capital + present value of future EVAs

While EVA has several purposes, its main use is as a period-by-period performance measurement where DCF valuation usually falls short. The EVA method is particularly useful in compensation programmes such as value-based management (VBM) programmes since EVA may be computed separately for different business units, departments, product lines or geographic business segments within the organization.

> The EVA and DCF models will generate the same value if the input data are consistent

It is a great strength that EVA provides a link between performance measurement and corporate valuation (Figure 4.4). This ensures evaluation and rewards to management and employees in a way consistent with how financial markets actually value companies. In this way, requirements of the

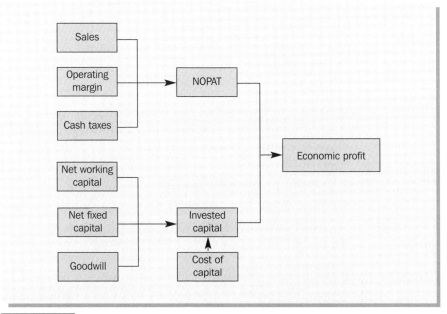

FIGURE 4.4 The link between performance measurement and corporate value

capital markets can be linked directly to operating performance measurements. For a further discussion on the use of EVA in incentive programmes, see Chapter 9, 'Value-based management'.

Valuations based on assets

Net asset valuation

This is perhaps the simplest form of company valuation. Basically, net asset valuation is the difference between the assets and liabilities based on their respective balance sheet values, adjusted for certain accounting principles. In other words, it is the adjusted value of the equity on the balance sheet (see Table 4.1).

Table 4.1: Balance sheet – Mobitronics

Assets		Liabilities and equity	
Goodwill	73	Equity	2,045
Net property, plant and equipment	2,771	Deferred income taxes	482
		Interest-bearing liabilities	245
Accounts receivable	971	Accounts payable and other liabilities	1,079
Operating cash	36		
Total assets	3,851	Total liabilities and equity	3,851

For example, the net asset value approach to valuing Mobitronics gives an equity value of 2,045m, far below the current market value in the stock market. A general observation is that this method often generates valuations below market value. In the autumn of 2009, net asset values accounted for only 29 per cent of the average value of a company on European stock markets. Apparently, the net asset value method is not congruent with how markets actually value companies.

The reason why net asset values are generally lower than market values is that many value-creating items are not accommodated in the balance sheet for accounting reasons. For example, investments in marketing, education of employees, R&D, etc. are generally not activated on the balance sheet but they all create value. The most extreme example is a consultancy; it may have very few tangible assets but can still be very valuable due to its people, brand name, processes, etc. In addition, accounting generally estimates asset values with caution. For example, computers are often written off in three years but they may still hold a value after that. However, the main source of the discrepancy between book values and market values is that the former do not take into account all future excess returns the management should be able to generate on these assets. We will have a more thorough discussion of this area in Chapter 7, 'Underlying analysis and key value drivers'.

Net asset valuation can be suitable for valuation of, for example, banks, real estate and investment companies

There are, however, certain industries where the net asset value method does give an accurate estimate of corporate value. Typically, this is when the company's future cash flows stem from squeezing a margin off the collective value of assets such as securities or real estate. Consequently, it can make sense to value banks, real estate and investment companies using the net asset value approach. For further insight into valuing these types of companies, see the Further reading section at the end of this book.

The most important relative valuation models: ratio-based valuation

As mentioned earlier, a valuation ratio expresses the value of a company in relation to another variable, for example sales, earnings or cash flow. That ratio can then be compared with those of other companies, the industry average or the company's own historical data. The terms 'ratio' and 'multiple' are used interchangeably as they refer to the same figure but the ratio is the outcome of a division exercise whereas the multiple is applied in multiplication.

A ratio or multiple expresses the value of a company in relation to a certain variable, for example earnings, EBIT or sales

The most common multiples are:

■ Earnings multiples where the company's value is put in relation to its current or forecasted net earnings. Since these are only available to the shareholders, they express the equity value. An example of an earnings multiple is price/earnings (P/E).

■ Cash flow and EBITDA multiples where the company's enterprise value is put in relation to its cash flow or operating profit (EBITDA), for example EV/EBITDA.

■ Revenue multiples where the company's value is put in relation to the company's revenues or sales. Since sales applies to all claimholders in the company, it expresses the enterprise value. An example of a revenue multiple is enterprise value/sales (EV/S).

▪ Asset multiples where the company's value is put in relation to its net asset value (also called book value) or adjusted net asset value, for example price/book value (P/BV).

▪ Operating multiples where the company's value is put in relation to some important operational value driver, for example number of customers, number of subscribers, etc. An example of an operating multiple is EV/customer.

We will go into further detail regarding ratio-based valuation and multiples in the next chapter.

Venture capital (VC) valuation

A specific form of valuation often used when valuing young firms is called VC valuation or 'target ownership approach'. The approach starts from the end by estimating an exit valuation and then calculating a value today based on the required returns for the investor. In its simplest form, the approach uses the following formula:

Post-money valuation = terminal value at exit year n/required ROI

where post-money valuation is the company value after the investment is made (post-money valuation = pre-money valuation + the capital invested), terminal value is the expected value of the company at an exit date at some point in the future and required ROI is the return the investor demands from investing in the specific company at this specific time.

The terminal value is the value you could expect the company to be worth at exit (an IPO or trade sale) in a few years from now. The terminal value can in theory be calculated using any valuation approach but in practice one or several multiples are often used and applied to the company's sales, earnings, etc.

Let's say that a company is expected to have sales of €30m in five years' time (usually the investors discount the revenues forecasted by management by 40–70 per cent) and that well-managed companies in the same industry have net margins of 10 per cent. If we assume the company will be able to reach the same margins then this would give net earnings of €3m in five years' time. If the most similar company has an earnings multiple (P/E) of 20 and if we apply this to the company being valued, we get a terminal value in five years' time of €60m (P/E 20 × €3m).

When applying another company's multiple, it is important to understand the circumstances surrounding that company's valuation:

■ Is the multiple from a listed company? Typically, a discount of approximately 30 per cent will be put on non-listed company valuations.

■ Is the valuation multiple based on an industrial acquisition of a company? If so, there might be a synergy component specific to that acquisition that cannot be applied to your company.

Venture capitalists and other early-stage investors generally demand very high returns on their investments. This is because early-stage investing is risky and many companies never even come close to revenues or earnings predicted in the business plan. Accordingly, investors never come close to the returns hoped for and in some companies might lose the entire investment. In a typical portfolio of 10 start-up companies, investors can expect three to five to fail completely and another three to four to give the investor his or her money back. Hence, the return for the entire portfolio typically comes from one or two companies that need to be very successful in order for the total portfolio return to be reasonable.

Generally, the risk decreases as the company matures. Depending on when the investment is considered, the discount rate in the early stages can vary between 30–70 per cent or, put differently, investors want a return of 10 to 30 times their investment capital at exit.

Using 20 × invested capital and our terminal value of €60m gives:

$$\text{Post-money valuation} = €60m/20 = €3m$$

If the entrepreneur were looking at raising €1m, this means that the investor, in order to meet the required ROI, would need to own 33 per cent of the company (€1m invested/€3m valuation).

In this example, we simplified matters by assuming that one financing round was all it was needed to bring the company to an exit. In reality, companies will often take several rounds of financing and each round dilutes the ownership of existing shareholders. Also, options might be offered to incentivize key employees which will further dilute the ownership at exit. Both these factors will affect the VC valuation but the basic concept remains the same.

This type of valuation is simplified and is made purely from the investor's perspective. It may be necessary to complement the VC valuation with other types of valuation. However, for an entrepreneur raising funds it can be valuable to understand how a professional early-stage investor may approach and evaluate an investment opportunity.

What models to use?

As can be seen, a large number of different valuation approaches exist. Which one should you then use? To a certain extent, this depends on the situation and your objectives (see Chapter 3). It also depends on which industry the company is active in, how mature the company is and how detailed the valuation should be.

An interesting fact to keep in mind is that, mathematically, most valuation models will yield similar results, given that the input data are consistent. For example, one can prove mathematically that, under certain assumptions, the five standalone valuation models (DDM, DCF, residual income, EVA and CFROI) presented in this chapter are, in all important aspects, equal.

The most common valuation approach, which we would also like to recommend in most cases, is to use the McKinsey version of the DCF model combined with a number of key ratios. The advantage of the DCF model is that it requires a good understanding of the underlying business, the value-creation opportunities and the key value drivers of the business. As mentioned earlier, DCF valuations tend to correspond very well to valuations observed in the marketplace.

However, the DCF approach also has its disadvantages. It is time-consuming and very sensitive to small errors in key input variables. That is why most valuation professionals combine the DCF valuation with the use of a number of suitable multiples. By doing this, the valuation can be checked for reasonableness. In addition, you should check the implicit long-term assumptions underlying the DCF model for the same reason; the explicit assumption may be reasonable, but the implicit assumptions regarding key financial performance may be unreasonable.

> Most valuation professionals combine the DCF valuation with the use of a number of suitable multiples

See 'Checking your assumptions' on page 94 for a detailed discussion of this topic. Our suggested valuation approach to the valuation can be described as in Figure 4.5.

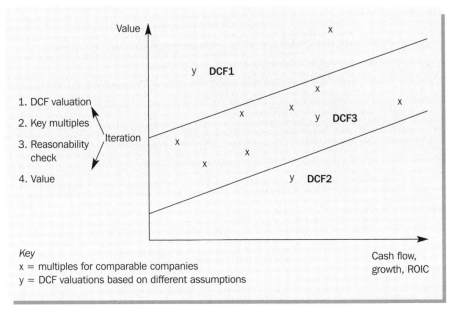

FIGURE 4.5   Our suggested valuation approach

How much focus should be put on ratios and how much on the stand-alone valuation often depends on how mature the company is. The more mature the company, the more focus should be put on the DCF valuation and vice versa. For small and/or new companies often only multiples are used. The focus in different stages of the company's lifecycle can be described as in Figure 4.6.

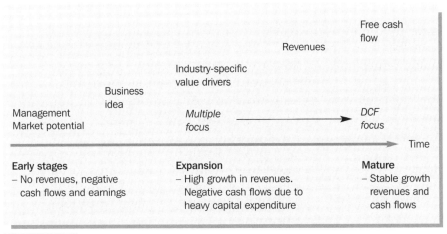

FIGURE 4.6   What is valued when (second time)

Summary

In this chapter we gave a theoretical overview of various important valuation concepts, such as equity value vs enterprise value and fundamental vs relative valuation. We then classified the valuation models according to these concepts (see Figure 4.3) and whether they are based on cash flow, returns or operational variables.

The most important and commonly used corporate valuation approaches are:

- **The discounted dividend model (DDM)** equals the equity value to the value of all future dividends discounted back to today using an appropriate cost of capital.

- **The discounted cash flow (DCF)** model equals the enterprise value to all future free cash flows discounted back to today using the appropriate cost of capital (usually the weighted average cost of capital (WACC)).

- **The cash flow return on investment (CFROI) model**: in contrast to the DCF, a return ratio is calculated that expresses the company's current or future ability to produce free cash flow. CFROI can be defined as the sustainable cash flow a business generates in a given year as a percentage of the cash invested in the company's assets.

- **Real options valuation**: where the basics of theoretical financial options pricing are used to price investment opportunities and ultimately companies. It is generally most applicable to companies whose value is strongly correlated to the success or failure of a certain opportunity. Examples of industries where real options valuation might be beneficial include energy (particularly oil and gas) and all R&D-intensive industries such as biotechnology, pharmaceutical and high-tech.

- **The residual income model** gives a value of the company based on the book value of the company plus the discounted value of all future excess returns after cost of debt and cost of equity have been deducted.

- **The economic value added (EVA) approach**: the enterprise value is equal to the current capital stock plus the present value of all future EVA, discounted back to today. EVA for a given year is the excess return the company enjoys, once all operating as well as capital costs are covered, and it is calculated as the difference between the return on capital and the cost of capital, multiplied by the capital stock at the beginning of the year.

▓ **The net asset valuation approach**: simply the difference between the assets and liabilities taken from the balance sheet, adjusted for certain accounting principles. In other words, it is the adjusted value of the equity on the balance sheet.

▓ **Ratio-based valuation**: the value of a company is expressed in relation to another company variable. That ratio can then be compared with those of other companies, the industry average or the company's own historical data.

▓ **Venture capital (VC) valuation** values the company from the investor's perspective based on an estimated terminal value at exit and the investor's required rate of return on invested capital.

Finally, we discussed that the most common valuation approach is using a DCF model in combination with a number of key valuation ratios. In the next chapter we will describe ratio-based valuation in more detail.

5

Ratio-based valuation

What topics are covered in this chapter?

- Classification of multiples
- Finding your multiple
- Different multiples
- How to find input data for multiple valuations
- Summary

Ratio-based valuations are frequently used by valuation experts, managers and investors. In ratio-based valuation (also called multiple-based valuation), the value of the company is expressed in relation to a specific variable such as sales, EBIT (earnings before interest and tax), net earnings or book value.

A ratio and a multiple refer to the same number but the terms are usually used in different contexts: ratio is the result of a division, value/variable = ratio; multiple is a term in a multiplication, variable × multiple = value.

**Remember:
ratio = multiple**

Classification of multiples

Fundamental and relative multiples

As mentioned in the previous chapter, there are two different ways to approach a multiple calculation and therefore two different types of multiple: fundamental and relative. Fundamental multiples are, as one might expect from the name, calculated based on company fundamentals. Relative multiples, by contrast, compare the relationship (the ratio) between the value of the company with a certain company variable, for example EBIT, with the same relationship for a similar company, the industry as a whole or historical data for the company. The most commonly used multiples are relative multiples.

In order to calculate a fundamental multiple the following steps need to be taken:

1 Identify an appropriate variable for valuing the company.

2 Find the necessary inputs for the calculation.

3 Adjust the numbers if needed.

4 Compute the ratio (for example, by using the formulas provided in this book).

5 Apply the multiple to estimate the company value or compare it with ratios for similar companies to view the relative value of the company.

And in order to calculate a relative multiple one needs to:

1 Identify an appropriate variable for valuing the company.

2 Find comparable companies or industry average data.

3 Adjust for differences between companies.

4 Calculate the ratio of the comparable companies or the industry.

5 Apply the ratio of comparable companies or industry average to a chosen company variable to estimate company value.

Equity and enterprise multiples

There are two basic types of multiple that can both be used as relative or fundamental multiples:

> The two basic types of multiple are relative and fundamental; both can be used to obtain enterprise and equity values

■ **Enterprise multiples** – express the value of the entire enterprise, enterprise value (EV), in relation to a variable that is relevant to all claimants (equity investors, lenders, minority interest holders, etc.) to the business. Typical multiples include EV/sales and EV/EBITDA.

- **Equity multiples** – express the value of the shareholders' claims on the business, generally called market value (MV) or simply price (P), in relation to a variable relevant only to the shareholders. These variables should be the residual left after creditors, minority interest holders and other non-equity claimants are paid. Equity value equals enterprise value less market value of debt, minority interests, pension provisions and other claims. Typical equity multiples are price/earnings and price/book values.

Note that it is important to be consistent and that both the value and the statistic chosen are relevant to the same claimholders in the firm.

Enterprise multiples are more comprehensive, more comparable and less affected by accounting than equity multiples

There are certain aspects of enterprise multiples that make them more appealing than equity multiples. Firstly, they are more comprehensive than equity multiples as they focus on the business as a whole rather than only the value of the claims of equity holders. Secondly, the enterprise multiples are less affected by capital structure differences because they measure the value of an unleveraged business. Finally, the EV multiples allow for use of statistics that are less affected by accounting differences, such as earnings before interest, taxes, depreciation and amortization (EBITDA) or operating free cash flow (OpFCF). A comparison between EBITDA and earnings, for example, shows that EBITDA is more comparable across companies and markets and consequently will need less adjustment.

When calculating an enterprise multiple, the statistic used must represent a flow available to all claimants. Earnings, for example, is only available to shareholders and may thus not be used as in an enterprise multiple. Sales, on the other hand, is available to all claimants and can be used. Roughly speaking, if a company is un-leveraged, i.e. has no debt, the enterprise value equals the equity since there are no other claimants (assuming no minority interests, pension interests, etc.).

Use of multiples

There are a number of ways to use multiples:

- Calculate the value of a specific company using another, similar company's or an industry average multiple. This is the standard way to use multiples.

- Comparison of a certain current multiple for a company with the same multiple for comparable companies. This is done either as part of a process of trying to assess the over/undervaluation of a business, or in order to understand what the market does or does not appreciate regarding companies in the sector. Often, one compares not only the multiple for the current year but also multiples based on the companies' forecasts and/or on historical data. Sometimes it may be interesting to analyze the spread between companies to see the post facto effects in valuation of, for example, strategic decisions or changes in capital structures.

Analyze the spread between companies to see the post facto effects in valuation

▪ Compare the current relative multiple assigned to a company by the market with a fundamental multiple, based on company fundamentals, as part of a process of trying to find undervalued or overvalued stocks. This analysis can be of special interest if the company being valued is in a sector that is currently in or out of favour in the investment community where the difference between the fundamental and the relative multiple for the company might be unreasonably high (see Figure 5.1).

▪ Forward multiples where the current market capitalization is put in relation to next year's forecasted sales, earnings or EBITDA, etc. Using projected numbers has the obvious drawback that estimations might not be accurate but they are, as we will come back to, more aligned with the theoretical value of a company and how markets actually value companies.

▪ Trailing multiples where numbers for the most recent available 12-month period is used. The benefit of this method versus the 'standard' multiple is that differences based on companies using different fiscal years are taken into consideration.

▪ Relative ratios are used to analyze a company's valuation in relation to the entire market. In terms of P/E, it can be expressed as: Relative P/E = P/E of firm ÷ P/E of market. It is of course important to use the same earnings measure, for example next year's earnings, to get meaningful results. Usually, relative ratios are compared over time.

Advantages/disadvantages of multiple-based valuation

There are a number of benefits to using multiples as a valuation tool:

▪ **Efficiency**. Using a multiple is often an expedient way to assess the value of a company, since the calculation of a multiple is usually uncomplicated and the data needed for a company or an industry average are easily available in the business press, in databases or through investment bank analyses. Compared for example with a full

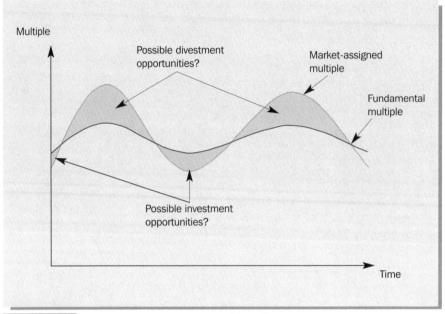

Multiple

Possible divestment
opportunities?

Market-assigned
multiple

Fundamental
multiple

Possible investment
opportunities?

Time

FIGURE 5.1   Relative vs fundametal multiple fluctuations

The principal benefits
of using multiples as a
valuation tool are that
it is efficient, significant
and complements other
methods

DCF analysis, it is a much faster and more conven-
ient valuation approach and the risk of making
technical mistakes is smaller. However, despite the
common perception that multiples are easy to calculate, calculating them correctly takes time and
effort, though a lot less so than a typical fundamental valuation.

■ **Significance.** If used correctly, using both fundamental and relative
multiples give a good assessment of the value of the company in question. In addition, investors commonly use multiples to analyze and
compare company values. That is why it is important to understand
and be able to discuss them. The nomenclature of the DCF model is
not as easily grasped and still not as widespread as that of ratios.

■ **Complementary function.** Doing a DCF or any other standalone
valuation is a rather cumbersome task and there is plenty of room for
mistakes. A quick way to check the reasonableness of the results from
such a valuation can be through comparison with suitable multiples.
In addition, it can be used as an acid test on a company in order to get
a quick understanding of the current valuation to decide whether time
should be spent on further analysis and valuation.

The criticism against multiples, on the other hand, is that they are:

▪ **Too simplistic**. A valuation multiple has to focus on only one variable and it may not accurately reflect other value-driving variables at play. For example, when doing a relative valuation of company B, if an EBIT multiple from comparable company A is used, a faster growth in the revenues of company B might be neglected. In other words, multiple valuations can miss company-specific value drivers (or value destroyers) and may not properly consider the operating or strategic dynamics in the underlying business.

▪ **Propensity for inaccuracy**. When conducting a relative multiple valuation, you are in fact letting other investors do the valuation for you. The multiple reflects what the market's opinion is on future cash flows, profits, margins, potential for growth and other important factors that influence the value of the company. What if the market and the other investors are all wrong? Also, there is often a need for adjustment of the variables used, which can be difficult to do accurately. Consequently, the accuracy of the valuation might suffer.

> The main drawbacks of multiples are that they can be too simplistic and rely on other investors' valuations

Finding your multiple

Picking the right one

Probably, the most important step in a multiple-based valuation is picking the right multiple or multiples. As always, when conducting a valuation, the focus is on identifying key variables that significantly affect corporate value. These variables can be anything from the apparent key variables, such as revenue or gross margin, to more operational and industry-specific variables, such as number of hotel rooms or number of kilowatt-hours (kWh) of electricity produced.

Multiple-based valuation is often used without enough understanding of a company's underlying business activities. This can lead to incorrect valuations and consequently incorrect investment decisions. Avoid this through a proper analysis of underlying key value drivers and the company's underlying business. We will discuss this further in Chapter 7, 'Underlying analysis and key value drivers'.

Analyzing comparability

Relative multiples produce a valuation of a company by applying the ratio for a certain variable from another company or the industry. It is important that these companies are similar to the company you are going to value. The multiple you aim to use should come from a company in a similar business and possess similar value drivers as the company you wish to value. But which companies are truly comparable? Some of the most important variables when seeking to compare similar companies are the following:

■ market size
■ market growth
■ relative market share
■ barriers to entry
■ brand strength
■ revenues
■ gross margins
■ growth in revenues and cash flow
■ capital expenditure level
■ operational and financial risk
■ capital structure.

In fact, to do a proper analysis, you need to examine each and every comparable company and try to understand also the underlying business drivers. Why are the multiples different in the peer group? Do certain companies have superior products, better access to key customers, recurring revenues, lower customer churn, etc? The more you understand the financial and operating specifics of each company in the peer group, the more meaningful the multiple analysis will be.

The truly diligent investor will then be sure to take into consideration all possible value-affecting differences between the companies. However, as always, there is a trade-off between economy of use and the grade of accuracy – you will have to decide on what adjustments are necessary. If there is no suitable, comparable company, it might be best to use the industry average.

We will address the considerations needed for the different multiples in more detail under the description of the various multiples.

Time period

When using multiples, one important question is which year's data should be used as a basis for the analysis? Theoretically, it is of course the future finances available to the company, and ultimately its future cash flows, that are of interest. Also, empirical studies have shown that forward-looking multiples more accurately determine company value and are more aligned with how companies are actually valued in the marketplace. These studies were, however, based on data from listed US-based companies where precise and accurate forecasts are more available than for most other companies, in many other markets. For smaller companies and companies without the pressure from the public stock market, forecasts tend to be less reliable. In practice therefore, most investors and analysts tend to look both at the most recent historical data as well as forecasts for the coming years. For example, when valuing our example company Mobitronics in 2010 using an EV/sales multiple, a common approach would be to take today's market capitalization, add net debt and divide this by the 2009, 2010, 2011 and 2012 sales respectively to obtain four different multiples. These ratios would then be compared with ratios from comparable companies as we try to examine whether the valuation is high or low. For example, the EV/sales ratios for companies comparable to Mobitronics in 2009 are shown in Figure 5.2.

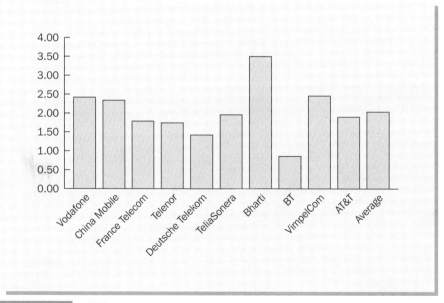

Another analysis that could be of interest when valuing your business is to look at historical multiples. For example, if you are looking to find an undervalued asset, you may not wish to compare only how today's market is valuing the future cash flows of your business and other similar businesses. It may also be of interest to understand how it has been valued historically. More specifically, it may be interesting to compare the current multiple valuation of a mature company with its valuation during the same stage in the last macroeconomic cycle. For instance, the graph of the historical P/E multiple for Microsoft Corporation is shown in Figure 5.3.

Suppose you find that today's multiple is below or above its historical average. This may say nothing about the future development of the stock, but it is nonetheless an interesting data point in your valuation of the company. If nothing fundamental has changed in the business or the industry, but the multiple has, either the historical multiple or the current one is incorrect.

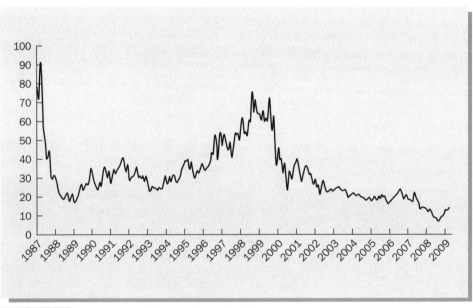

FIGURE 5.3   Microsoft P/E ratio (1987–2009)

The issue of accounting differences

Generally, in choosing your multiples, you wish to make the key statistics as comparable as possible. A number that is highly influenced by accounting will require more adjustments before it is comparable than those statistics that are less influenced. For example, profit multiples such as P/E ratios are very sensitive to accounting principles. If you compare the P/E ratios of two identical companies, where one company writes off assets at twice the speed of its competitor, the analysis regarding the two companies' relative valuations will be completely misleading. In general, accounting that does not affect cash flow does not and should not affect value.

The most common adjustments to consider for differences in accounting principles are shown in Table 5.1. These are just a few out of many accounting items you could compare and account for in order to achieve maximum comparability. However, as mentioned before, you need to decide how exact you wish the multiple to be. In many cases, an approximation might be sufficient.

Table 5.1: Common adjustments needed

Item	Issue
Amortization and depreciation	Do the companies you are comparing have the same time period as basis for write-off? Do they use the same principles?
Investments	Some companies may account for a certain type of capital outflow as a cost while others will define it as an investment in the balance sheet. This will affect the profit and must be accounted for.
Extraordinary items	Should generally be excluded from the calculations.
Leases	The basic but important difference that needs to be accounted for is whether the asset is included in the balance sheet as an investment purchased or off the balance sheet as rented.

One way to avoid some of these pitfalls is to use other statistics less influenced by accounting standards. This usually means calculating enterprise value instead of equity value. Certainly, this will depend on why you are carrying out the valuation and whether you think calculating enterprise value will give rise to more complexities than the accounting differences will. But, if an enterprise valuation suits your purposes, there are a number of statistics to choose from which are less influenced by accounting. These include:

■ **Sales (revenues).** As the top line of the income statement, sales tend to be comparable between companies and even between markets. However, sales do not consider any of the costs involved in the business and do not give any measure of profitability. Also, caution needs to be taken since sales are not completely unaffected by accounting differences. In particular, differences in the handling of recognized and deferred revenues can be an issue.

■ **EBITDA (earnings before interest and tax, depreciation and amortization).** This item appears further down in the income statement and covers most costs in a company, and is a decent measure of profitability. It is also largely unaffected by accounting differences (often the two major accounting effects on EBITDA are how sales and costs are recognized). As it is also a good approximation of cash flow, EBITDA is one of the most commonly used statistics in multiple valuation today.

■ **Cash flow.** This is, when calculated correctly, a statistic completely unaffected by accounting measures. Even cash flow may be 'massaged' by overly creative managers, see Enron for example, but it is still generally highly suitable for a multiple comparison. The downside is the complexity of calculating cash flow correctly and that cash flow may be very volatile from year to year due to extraordinary revenues, costs or investments. Therefore, one sometimes uses trend cash flow over a number of years in order to adjust for abnormal cash in- and outflow.

Different multiples

Below, we will present and calculate some of the most used and useful multiples, and discuss their pros and cons and when they should be used.

Book value (BV) multiples

■ A book value multiple reflects the market value of the equity in relation to the company's book value. It is basically what would be left over for shareholders if the company was shut down and its debt paid back. Book value is the adjusted book value of total assets, less adjusted book value of liabilities. The ratio is called the price/book value or P/BV ratio and in some countries net asset value (NAV) ratio.

The formula for the relative multiple is:

$$\frac{\text{Price}}{\text{BV}} = \frac{\text{market capitalization}}{\text{adjusted BV of total assets} - \text{adjusted BV of liabilities}}$$

A book value multiple reflects the market value of the equity in relation to the company's book value

In the early days of valuation in the first half of the 20th century, the price/book value was widely used and was much more popular than it is today. That is because it works best with a company with a lot of tangible assets like factories, hardware, commodities, mines, etc. and that derives its revenues and cash flow from those assets. Examples of such companies today are banks, real estate and investment companies. All these industries have a common denominator in that they squeeze a small margin off a large asset base. Figure 5.4 illustrates the price relative book value in different industries.

However, many companies today rely heavily on intellectual assets and derive their revenues and cash flows from those intellectual assets. These companies often have relatively low book values, which makes the price/book value ratio unsuitable for valuation.

The formula for the fundamental multiple is:

$$\frac{\text{Price}}{\text{BV}} = \frac{\text{ROE} - g}{\text{ROE} \times (C_E - g)} \times \text{ROE}$$

where ROE is return on equity, g is earnings growth and C_E is the cost of equity.

As can be seen from the fundamental formula, the return on equity (ROE) will to a large extent determine the P/BV ratio. A high ROE should normally result in a high P/BV ratio as investor demand will increase for a share giving them a good return on equity. A low ROE should, on the other hand, normally result in a low P/BV ratio as investor demand decreases for a share with a low return on equity. Similarly, a high earnings growth rate should lead to a higher P/BV ratio and a lower growth rate to a lower P/BV ratio.

When calculating the P/BV ratio for a company in distress, usually all intangible assets are removed from the book value since they most probably have no resale value. That ratio is sometimes referred to as price/tangible book value and is computed as:

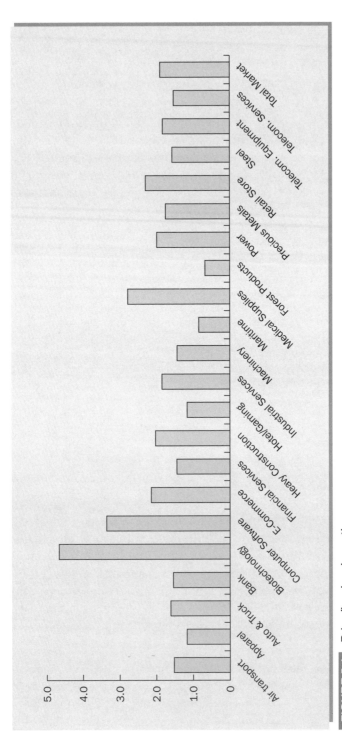

FIGURE 5.4 Price/book value ratios

$$P/\text{Tangible book value} = \frac{\text{market capitalization}}{\text{BV of assets} - \text{book value of liabilities} - \text{BV of intangible assets}}$$

The main benefits of the price/book value multiple are as follows:

- It is a fairly intuitive concept that is easily understood and the numbers needed are easily found in the company's balance sheet.
- Book value is often fairly stable over time and thus suitable for historical analysis.
- It can be used at times when companies are making losses or producing negative cash flows. Since assets are defined similarly in most markets/countries, comparisons work relatively well with P/BV ratios.

The major drawback with P/BV ratios is that they assume that net assets are the key source to value creation. For many companies today, including all service firms with no significant assets, this is not correct. Other drawbacks include:

- Book values are highly affected by accounting principles. As such, book values may differ significantly between companies or countries and may not be comparable.
- The book value on the balance sheet may not reflect the real economic value of the asset at all and the market value might be a completely different one.

Revenue multiples

A revenue multiple (also called sales multiple) reflects the value of the enterprise in relation to its revenues (sales). Since revenue is a money stream available to all claimholders in the firm, it must be put in relation to the company's enterprise value. Thus, the commonly used multiple price/sales which relates sales to the equity value (generally expressed as price) is in fact theoretically incorrect and should only be used when enterprise value is equal to equity value.

A revenue multiple (also called a sales multiple) reflects the value of the enterprise in relation to its revenues (sales) = EV/S

When using a revenue multiple, no form of the company's profitability or cash flow is taken into consideration, which means that the company's value is not put in relation to any key variable for theoretical value (cash flow, EBIT, etc.). Therefore, when using a revenue multiple, you indirectly make strong assumptions about the company's cost structure, and revenue multiples are strongly dependent on the operating margins and higher (lower) EV/S ratios will almost always be accompanied with high (low) operating margins. In fact, it can be said that only companies with similar cost structures and operating margins can be properly compared.

Since no measurement of the company's profitability is needed, revenue multiples can be and often are used to value loss-making companies.

$$\frac{EV}{sales} = \frac{enterprise\ value}{sales}$$

EV/sales can also be expressed as a fundamental multiple. The formula for the fundamental multiple is:

$$\frac{EV}{sales} = \frac{ROIC - g}{ROIC \times (WACC - g)} \times (1-T) \times M$$

where ROIC is return on invested capital, g is revenue growth, WACC is weighted average cost of capital, T is the tax rate and M is EBITDA margin in per cent.

And for price/sales

$$\frac{Price}{sales} = \frac{profit\ margin \times payout\ ratio \times (1+g)}{C_E - g}$$

where payout ratio is calculated as dividend/earnings, g is growth rate and C_E is the cost of equity.

So when is it appropriate to use revenue multiples? As mentioned, revenue multiples are rough measures, but they have a number of important advantages:

- Revenues are relatively hard to manipulate for management, unlike many other statistics, and are largely unaffected by accounting decisions on inventory, depreciation, extraordinary charges, etc. Therefore, they can easily be compared between companies, industries or countries.

- While most other variables can be or become negative and thereby impossible to use for multiples, revenue variables work for most firms in most stages and situations. Many newly started companies post a loss at all levels of their income statements. Also, many troubled firms may have negative numbers at least at some level of the income statement. This means that neither cash flow nor earnings ratios can be used, as they require a positive denominator, while the revenue multiple is still applicable.

■ Revenue multiples tend to be more stable over time and are less affected by extraordinary items than earnings or, particularly, cash flow. Therefore, they might more accurately present the company's long-term trend than any other measure and thereby be reliable for use in valuations.

■ Changes in pricing policies, increased competition or strategic decisions often affect revenues first, so revenues may also give a good indication of the future situation for companies or industries in change.

Things to watch out for when using revenue multiples include sales volatility, revenue recognition policies and margin differences between compared companies.

Normally, revenue multiples relate strongly to the company's revenue growth; the higher the revenue growth, the higher the multiple. Also, as mentioned previously, revenue multiples are directly related to margins. All other things being equal, higher margins lead to higher multiples. This knowledge can be used as a tool when trying to identify possible investment opportunities, as shown in Figure 5.5.

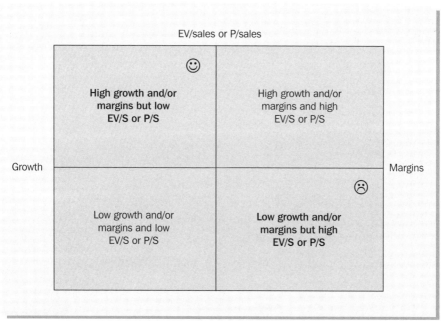

FIGURE 5.5   What to look for when analyzing investment objects

Earnings multiples

The price/earnings (P/E) multiple expresses the value of the equity in relation to its earnings after tax. This multiple is probably the most used and quoted among all multiples and was introduced as early as the 1930s. It is still popular despite the fact that most professionals agree that earnings are not the optimal measurement of a company's financial performance. The formula for the relative multiple can be expressed as:

$$\frac{\text{Price}}{\text{earnings}} = \frac{\text{market capitalization}}{\text{net income}}$$

or alternatively on a share basis:

$$\text{Price/earnings} = \text{share price/earnings per share}$$

The price/earnings (P/E) multiple expresses the value of the equity in relation to its earnings after tax

Let's say that company XYZ has earnings after tax of €10m and is currently trading in the stock market at a total market capitalization of €150m. The P/E would then be 150/10 = 15.

The measure is a residual, only taking into account flows to the equity investors. As it comes last in the income statement, it is heavily influenced by accounting principles.

The formula for the fundamental version of a P/E multiple can be expressed as:

$$\frac{\text{Price}}{\text{earnings}} = \frac{\text{ROE} - g}{\text{ROE} \times (C_E - g)}$$

where ROE is return on equity, g is earnings growth rate and C_E is the cost of equity. As can be seen from the formula, the P/E ratio is mainly dependent on three variables: ROE, g and C_E.

P/E multiples for a number of industries can be found in Figure 5.6.

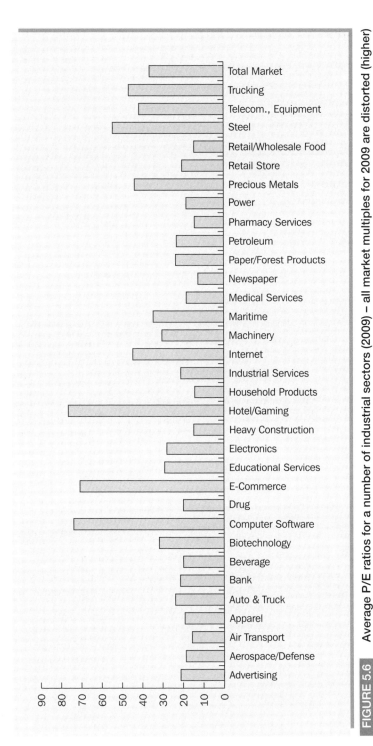

FIGURE 5.6   Average P/E ratios for a number of industrial sectors (2009) – all market multiples for 2009 are distorted (higher) due to the financial crisis

Earnings ratios are highly sensitive to accounting decisions because of the place of profits at the very end of the income statement. They are best used when the current earnings are representative of future earnings and the earnings trend. The main reasons behind the multiples' popularity and their principal benefits are:

- Intuitively appealing statistic that relates the price paid for an asset to its earnings.
- The data for its computation are readily available. Historical, current and forecasted earnings for most public companies are public and easy to gain access to.
- A rather concrete measure of what is available for distribution to the shareholders.
- Commonly used, it is often mentioned in the business press, it is known by investors, etc. Most investors have an idea of what a high or low P/E multiple is, which increases its use and makes it easy to discuss.

There are, however, a number of important disadvantages in using P/E ratios:

- They are susceptible to accounting measures. This can be somewhat avoided by adding back goodwill amortization and exceptional items, but this still leaves room for manipulation.
- They do not explicitly take into consideration cost for future growth; a firm with high growth will normally have a higher multiple, even though it might give less return on equity, as it requires more capital to achieve that growth.
- Earnings multiples are more likely than cash flow multiples to reflect market moods and perceptions regarding entire sectors. This makes them more likely to be part of systematic errors.

Figure 5.7 shows the development of the P/E ratios of the S&P 500 companies since 1880.

Companies with high P/E ratios are typically high growth stocks since all other factors being equal, the higher the growth, the higher the P/E multiple. However, their relatively high multiples do not necessarily mean their stocks are overpriced or overvalued. The question is – how much higher P/E is justified by a certain difference in growth rate? Or, put differently, how much is a certain growth rate worth? To examine the relationship between the growth rate and the P/E ratio, we need to factor the growth rate into the P/E equation, obtaining the so-called PEG ratio.

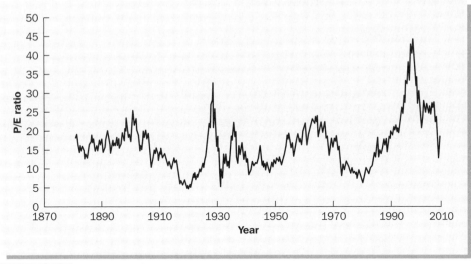

FIGURE 5.7   P/E ratios of the S&P 500 companies since 1880, based on the average inflation adjusted earnings of the previous ten years

PEG ratio

The PEG ratio can be expressed as:

$$PEG = \frac{P/E \text{ ratio}}{\text{projected annual growth rate in earnings}}$$

- A PEG factor equal to 1 means that the market is pricing the stock to reflect fully its earnings per share growth potential.
- A PEG factor greater than 1 indicates that either the stock is overvalued or that the market expects its future earnings per share growth to be greater than the current forecast.
- A PEG factor less than 1 indicates that either the stock is undervalued or that the market does not expect the company to achieve its forecasted earnings per share growth.

In fact, the PEG ratio expresses how much you will have to pay for each unit of future earnings growth. Therefore, the PEG ratio is often of great explanatory value when examining the P/E ratio. A P/E ratio of 30 with a forecasted growth rate of 15 per cent (PEG = 2) is more attractive than a P/E ratio of 7 with 2 per cent (PEG = 3.5) forecasted growth.

Let's say you are considering buying stocks in the growth superstar company of the last decade – Google. At the time of writing, Google is trading at a P/E multiple of 47. A quick comparison with the NASDAQ average P/E ratio of 30 could make you conclude that Google could be overvalued in relation to the market. Introducing the growth rate changes the picture completely since Google, with its expected earnings growth rate of 33 per cent, has a PEG ratio of 1.40 compared with the average expected growth rate of the NASDAQ of 15 per cent, resulting in a PEG ratio of 2. Using the PEG ratio instead suggests that Google is undervalued compared to the market.

The PEG ratio provides more insight about a stock's current valuation than the traditional P/E ratio. The relationship between the P/E ratio and earnings growth tells a much more complete story than the P/E on its own.

The main drawback with the PEG ratio, however, is that it is very sensitive to forecasts on growth rates.

EBITDA multiples

An EBITDA multiple expresses the enterprise value in relation to the most cash flow-like measurement in the income statement, EBITDA. The measure is a proxy of cash flow and has important advantages over cash flow in that it is found easily in the income statement and it is more stable over time. It is probably the most commonly used EV multiple among professional investors due to its resemblance to cash flow and that the appropriate data are easy to find.

> An EBITDA multiple expresses the enterprise value in relation to the most cash flow-like measurement in the income statement, EBITDA

The formula for the fundamental EBITDA multiple can be expressed as:

$$\frac{EV}{EBITDA} = \frac{ROIC - g}{ROIC \times (WACC - g)} \times (1 - T) \times (1 - D)$$

where ROIC is return on invested capital, g is growth, WACC is weighted average cost of capital, T is the tax rate and D is depreciation charges in per cent of EBITDA.

And the formula for the relative multiple is:

$$\frac{EV}{EBITDA} = \frac{\text{market value of equity + market value of net debt + minority interests + pension provisions + other claims}}{EBITDA}$$

The EBITDA variable is more affected by accounting measures than revenues, but it is still largely unaffected and certainly less affected than, for example, earnings. Other key benefits of an EBITDA multiple include:

■ As with the revenue multiple, it can be used on firms currently reporting net losses (as long as the company has positive EBITDA).

■ When used to estimate corporate value, it approaches a DCF valuation as it is an approximation of cash flow.

■ By examining cash inflows to the entire firm prior to debt payments, it allows for comparisons between firms with different debt leverage.

■ As it resembles cash flow, it is a good tool when evaluating acquisitions, for example in leveraged buyouts.

When using EBITDA multiples it is, however, important to keep in mind that:

■ Even though EBITDA resembles cash flow, it is not exactly the same. For example, it does not take into consideration tax payments or changes in working capital. These variables may increase or decrease corporate value but are not visible in the EBITDA.

■ Required future investments heavily affect cash flow and value but are not included in an EBITDA calculation.

■ It can only be used when EBITDA is positive (unless you normalize the EBITDA using historical and/or future numbers).

As can be seen from the formula for the fundamental multiple, the EBITDA multiple is affected by, for example:

■ **Tax level** – the higher the tax level, the lower the multiple. Skilled tax management can produce higher than normal multiples.

■ **Cost of capital** – the riskier the business or the financial structure, the higher the cost of capital. Higher cost of capital means lower valuation. Even a firm with low leverage, but with high operational risk, will be punished with a lower multiple.

- **Depreciation** – as depreciation increases, given that the capital expenditure does not follow, the multiple will increase, partly due to positive tax effects.
- **Growth and capital expenditure** – if a company can generate growth more efficiently than comparable companies and/or spend less capital, the multiple will be higher.

Operating free cash flow (OpFCF) multiples

OpFCF multiples reflect the value of the entire enterprise in relation to its operating free cash flow. There are a number of different cash flow multiples to choose from, ranging from pure cash flow to approximations taken from the income statement such as NOPAT or EBITDA. Pure free cash flow, suitable for discounted cash flow valuations, has major drawbacks when used for multiple valuation since it has a tendency to fluctuate significantly from year to year due to infrequent capital expenditures and extraordinary items. It may also be difficult to estimate a reasonable level of what is called trend cash flow. EBITDA and NOPAT, on the other hand, carry the drawback of being somewhat 'accounting sensitive'. A reasonable middle way is to use what is called operating free cash flow as a basis.

Calculate operating free cash flow as EBITDA less estimated annual required reinvestment and less inflation on working capital needed. The formula for an OpFCF fundamental multiple can be expressed as:

$$\frac{EV}{OpFCF} = \frac{ROIC - g}{ROIC \times (WACC - g)} \times (1 - T)$$

where ROIC is calculated as OpFcF/capital stock, g is growth, WACC is weighted average cost of capital, and T is taxes.

The formula for the relative multiple is:

$$\frac{EV}{OpFCF} = \frac{\text{equity value + market value of net debt + minority interests + pension provisions + other claims}}{\text{EBITDA – annual reinvestment – inflation on working capital}}$$

OpFCF is comparable to a normalized EBIT or a smoothed cash flow. As such, it will provide a good basis for multiple valuation that should reflect fairly accurately the value according to a DCF calculation. The main benefits of the multiple include:

▪ OpFCF is less affected by accounting distortions than other cash flow estimations such as EBIT or EBITDA.

▪ As a cash flow multiple, it allows for good comparisons across different companies.

▪ As the OpFCF measure is less volatile than FCF, it becomes more suited for historical comparisons and trend analysis.

The 'only' disadvantages are that:

▪ As with all the other mentioned multiples, the denominator, in this case OpFCF, must be positive. If negative, a normalized OpFCF can be used instead.

▪ It is rather complex to calculate.

Operational multiples

Operational multiples express the value of the company in relation to a specific operational statistic, often a revenue-related capacity measure of some sort. These are usually specific to a certain industry or industry segment. The variable used in the multiple should always be a key revenue and cash flow driver. Some examples of operational multiples from different industries are shown in Table 5.2.

Table 5.2: Operational multiples from different industries

Industry	Multiple
Media	EV/number of subscribers
Energy	EV/kWh production capacity
Accommodation	EV/number of hotel rooms
Telecommunications	EV/number of mobile (fixed line, broadband, internet) subscribers
E-commerce	EV/number of members (customers)

Operational multiples express the value of the company in relation to a specific operational statistic, often a revenue-generating unit of some sort

It is possible to produce a large number of more or less usable ratios for a certain industry, but it is essential to understand what drives growth in the industry and what is going to create free cash flows and value in the end. The difficult task is not to calculate the ratios but rather to understand the industry and which key operational value drivers to focus on.

A general formula for a fundamental multiple can be written as:

$$\frac{EV}{unit} = \frac{ROIC - g}{ROIC \times (WACC - g)} \times \frac{NOPAT}{unit}$$

where ROIC is return on invested capital, g is growth, WACC is weighted average cost of capital, NOPAT is net operating profit after tax and unit is the unit appropriate for the company and industry under analysis.

For a relative multiple, a general formula is:

$$\frac{EV}{unit} = \frac{\text{market value of equity + market value of net debt + minority interests + pension provisions + other claims}}{\text{number of capacity or revenue-generating units}}$$

Often, operative multiples are used to get an early indicator of key business elements or to evaluate the outcome of a firm's strategic decisions. For example, a media company deciding on a different marketing strategy might build a subscriber base that does not immediately affect revenues in the income statement but is expected to do so in the future. Consequently, using the number of subscribers or growth in number of subscribers as a proxy for coming revenues can give an early indication of what is to come.

Another use is to understand the value created in early phases of projects or businesses. The operative multiple can give early insights regarding the future revenue and cash flow potential.

Operative multiples are also used to compare the implied value of productive assets (such as kWh) for comparison between firms in an industry or segment. This value can also be compared with the replacement cost. This ratio is called Tobin's Q, and is defined as the ratio between the market value of assets in an economy or company and the replacement cost of

Tobin's Q is the ratio
between the market
value of assets in an
economy or company
and the replacement
cost of those assets

those assets. This measure can be a useful tool in identifying acquisition opportunities. For example, if the market is valuing an industry's assets lower than its replacement cost, then a company in that industry has an incentive to acquire assets through the stock market rather than buying them more expensively on the goods market.

There are, however, a number of difficulties and pitfalls in using operative multiples:

▪ These multiples do not generally provide enough information to assess appropriately the value of a company. There are a large number of implicit assumptions regarding how the variable in question will generate value. For example, we might not know what margins will be applicable for a certain product or service and hence it may be difficult to estimate the cash flow (and the value) a subscriber base will generate.

▪ An operative multiple only roughly approximates value since what drives a company's value is not its assets, but its use of those assets to create economic value. There are an indefinite number of management decisions left out when using operational multiples.

▪ Differences in strategy, pricing, margins or any other factor may motivate large differences in multiples for different companies within the same industry.

How to find input data for multiple valuations

In order to carry out a fundamental multiple valuation all you need is the financial data for the year in question. These data are normally available on the company's website or in its annual reports.

In order to perform relative multiple valuations, you need to know how the market is valuing a comparable company or the industry average. You can find these numbers in the business press, in analyst reports on financial websites or in selective databases. In addition, as you will often find the market capitalization of a company on the website of the stock exchange where the stock is traded, you can do the calculations yourself based on the company's own projections.

Summary

In this chapter, we described ratio-based valuation, also called multiple-based valuation. Multiples are classified as either enterprise multiples where a certain variable is related to the company's enterprise value or equity multiples where a certain variable is related to the company's equity value. There is also a distinction between fundamental multiples based on company fundamentals and relative multiples based on another company's or the average industry figures. The main advantage of multiples is that they are simple to use and yet produce a reasonably accurate value assessment. The main disadvantages are that they can miss company-specific value drivers and always rely on a value assessment of the company or the industry carried out by others (relative multiples).

We explained the importance in choosing a similar company in relative valuations and taking into consideration important differences in growth, capital structure or margins.

We then moved into a presentation of some of the most commonly used multiples:

▪ **Book value multiples** value the equity (price) in relation to the company's book value of equity. Generally, book values are not good estimations of value. In some industries, however, where tangible assets are key to the company's future revenues and cash flows, book value multiples can be useful. Such industries include banks, real estate companies and investment companies.

▪ **Revenue** or **sales multiples** should be expressed as an enterprise multiple (EV/sales) and not as an equity multiple (P/sales) which is often the case. Revenue multiples can be used when valuing young ventures or companies with negative cash flow, EBITDA and profit since these variables cannot be used if they are negative.

▪ **Earnings multiples**. The P/E ratio relates the company's earnings to its equity value (price) and is still the most commonly used multiple today. The P/E ratio is easy to understand and fairly simple to calculate since the company's current or forecasted earnings are easily observed in most cases. Also, almost everyone has an opinion regarding P/E ratios and thus they are easy to discuss. However, P/E ratios are heavily influenced by accounting and do not necessarily give a good indication of a company's cash flow.

▪ **The PEG ratio** is a combination of the P/E ratio and forecasted growth in annual earnings. The PEG ratio gives an indication of how the company is valued based on P/E in relation to its earnings growth and can be used to compare the valuations of two companies with different growth rates.

▪ **EBITDA multiples** express the enterprise value (EV) in relation to the company's EBITDA. EBITDA is the most cash flow-like measurement in a company's income statement. It approximates a company's cash flow, without the difficulties of calculating a pure cash flow. Therefore, it is probably the most used multiple among professional investors. It is important to note, however, that even though a valuation based on an EBITDA multiple approaches one based on a cash flow, it ignores other important aspects such as changes in working capital.

▪ **Operating free cash flow multiples** reflect the value of the entire enterprise (EV) in relation to its operating free cash flow. Operating free cash flow is more cash flow-like than EBITDA. However, it needs to be calculated and cannot be observed in the income statement. This is a multiple that, if used correctly, will best indicate a true value of the company's future cash flow.

▪ **Operational multiples** express the value of the company in relation to a specific operational statistic, often a capacity measure of some sort. Usually these are specific to a certain industry or industry segment and it is of utmost importance that the multiple is a key driver of cash flow, thus affecting the value of the company. Often, operative multiples are used to get an early indicator of the development of a young business or to evaluate the outcome of strategic decisions of a firm.

In the following chapter we will present the McKinsey version of the DCF model and show how to use it for company valuation.

6

Discounted cash flow valuation

What topics are covered in this chapter?

- Estimating the cost of capital – WACC
- Calculating free cash flow
- Computing terminal value
- Discounting and final corporate value
- The most important variables in a DCF analysis
- The DCF approach – only a calculation machine
- Checking your assumptions
- Summary

> The most commonly used standalone valuation model is the discounted cash flow (DCF) model

The most commonly used standalone valuation model is the discounted cash flow (DCF) model. There are many different types of DCF model. Of these, the most frequently used is the so-called McKinsey model, which was first presented in 1990 by Tom Copeland, Tim Koller and Jack Murrin in the book *Valuation – measuring and managing the value of companies*. This work has become something of a bible in DCF valuation and we recommend it for those who wish to have a deeper understanding of the McKinsey model than this book allows.

The McKinsey version of the DCF model is a specific type of standalone valuation model. Other models also exist, such as economic value added (EVA), proposed by the consulting firm Stern & Stewart, and cash flow return on investment (CFROI), developed by the HOLT Value Consultants. These models are in many ways similar to the McKinsey model and, under certain assumptions, can be shown to be completely consistent with it. In this book, we will concentrate on and present the McKinsey model in more detail. This is because it is the most used by valuation professionals and has been proven to work well in a large number of industries and different valuation situations.

The main idea behind the McKinsey model (and all other cash flow models) is that the value of a company today is equal to all future free cash flows, discounted back to the present with a discount rate that reflects the level of risk inherent in those cash flows. In other words, you need to estimate and calculate all future free cash flows, year by year, and estimate the level of risk associated with these cash flows (i.e. calculate a discount rate) and discount the future cash flows back to today.

Why, then, have cash flow models in general, and the McKinsey model in particular, become so popular and widely used? There are a number of reasons for this:

▪ The model is theoretically 'correct' and is compatible with financial theory and other models used on the capital markets, for example the capital asset pricing model (CAPM) and the time value of money. The fact that the majority of financial academics advocate the model obviously gives it considerable weight.

▪ Company valuations produced by the DCF model fit very well with the way capital markets value companies in practice. Valuation models produce a theoretical value of a company and, if that company is traded publicly, you have a practical value of the company with which to compare. Certainly, for a valuation model to be useful, it must, to a certain extent, correspond to valuations on the financial market.

▪ In theory the DCF model works well for all companies, from the smallest high-growth companies to mature multinationals.

▪ The DCF model is less sensitive to so-called window dressing, i.e. when accounts are manipulated or altered to improve figures. Since the DCF model focuses on cash flows, any accounting measures that do not affect cash flows do not affect the DCF model.

▪ The DCF model requires an understanding of the underlying business and the industry within which the company operates. This means that the person performing the valuation will need to investigate the basic factors that create and drive value in the company and industry. This is not required to the same extent when, for example, performing a valuation based on relative multiples or net assets, which consequently can lead to mistakes due to a lack of insight.

It is important to remember that earnings could be but do not have to be a proxy of cash flow. As we have mentioned, earnings are affected by various accounting measures, as exemplified in Table 6.1.

Table 6.1: Earnings do not necessarily reflect cash flow

Fiscal year 2009	H&M	Coca-Cola	IBM	AstraZeneca
Earning per share (EPS)	19.8	2.95	10.01	5.19
Cash flow per share (FCF)	11.14	1.75	10.55	7.28
FCF/EPS	56%	59%	105%	140%

Before looking more closely at the DCF model, it is important to mention that the model itself should be regarded as a calculator – it is a machine that will produce a value based solely on your inputs and it can produce any value you wish. Therefore, the major difficulty in performing a DCF valuation is not constructing the model, but rather deciding on the input variables regarding the company's and the sector's future prospects. This is the principal challenge, even for valuation professionals with extensive experience of company valuation. Therefore, when conducting a DCF valuation, spend considerable time and care on the so-called underlying analysis.

> When conducting a DCF valuation, spend considerable time and care on the so-called underlying analysis

The following presentation of the standard McKinsey DCF model is divided into four main sections:

1 Estimating the cost of capital – WACC.
2 Calculating free cash flow.
3 Computing terminal value.
4 Discounting and final corporate value.

Estimating the cost of capital – WACC

As mentioned earlier, the value of an enterprise according to the DCF model is based on the sum of all future discounted free cash flows. Consequently, the first thing we need to do is calculate the cost of capital with which we will discount these cash flows. The so-called *discount rate* should reflect the risk inherent in the forecasted future cash flows. Various methods of calculating a company's cost of capital exist, but the weighted average cost of capital (WACC) is the most used today. The WACC is calculated using the following formula:

The cost of capital with which the cash flows are discounted should reflect the risk inherent in the future cash flows

$$WACC = \frac{E}{D+E} \times C_E + \frac{D}{D+E} \times C_D \times (1-T)$$

where E is market value of equity, D is market value of debt, C_E is the cost of equity, C_D is the cost of debt and T is the tax rate.

WACC is a reasonably theoretically correct method to calculate the cost of capital and its calculation can be separated into three parts:

1 Assessment of the target capital structure.
2 Calculation of the cost of capital for equity financing.
3 Calculation of the cost of capital for non-equity financing.

Target capital structure

The term 'capital structure' refers to how the company has financed its operations, which generally can be done through internally generated cash, equity or debt. The focus in the analysis of the capital structure is the debt/equity ratio of the company.

The board of directors and management usually have two diametrically opposite factors to take into consideration when determining the debt/equity ratio. On the one hand, debt carries lower risk and is therefore normally cheaper than equity and therefore an attractive source of financing. The interest on the debt is often by itself lower than the demanded return on equity. In addition, interest expenses are most often tax deductible. Therefore, the more debt, the lower the average cost of capital and

The term 'capital structure' refers to how the company has financed its operations thus a higher return on equity. On the other hand, the management needs to balance operational risk versus financial risk. If you are running an early-stage high-tech company, the operational risk is normally high and the cash flow very volatile, and you therefore want to avoid increased financial risk by adding debt to the balance sheet. This balancing act is often quite industry specific and common knowledge. For example, real estate companies normally have quite high leverage (as the operational risk is quite low), whereas fashion companies with high operational risk have lower leverage. Figure 6.1 shows the capital structures in different industries.

The first step in determining the WACC is to assess the company's target capital structure. This is done through estimation based on four inputs:

1 The current capital structure based on market values.

2 Capital structures of comparable companies.

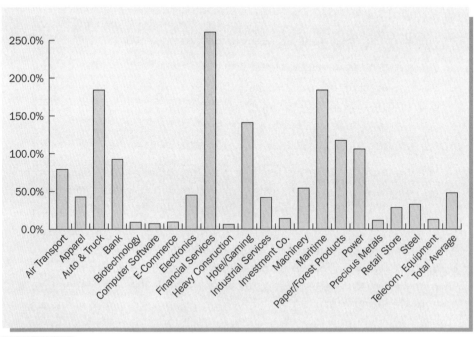

FIGURE 6.1   D/E ratios based on market values (Q1 2010)

3 The likely future capital structure based on the financing policies and corporate strategy of the management.

4 The capital structure that achieves the lowest possible WACC while providing enough interest coverage and a beneficial balance between operative and financial risk.

The current capital structure should be calculated using market values of the different types of capital, and not through book values. This is an uncomplicated and reasonably accurate procedure in cases when the equity and bonds issued by the company are publicly traded. However, in many cases market values are not public. In such cases, a number of different approaches are available.

The first thing to look for is a recent debt or equity transaction made by the company for an indication of the market value of the debt or the equity; if the transaction is recent, this will provide a good approximation of market value. Another way to estimate the market value of debt is to calculate the net present value of all future payments on the debt, including the full repayment of the debt.

You should also review capital structures of similar companies. If there are large differences between current capital structures for companies in the industry, you will need to understand why. Factors influencing differences could be dissimilar operative risks due to aggressive expansion strategies, financially conservative management or a number of other reasons. The input is nonetheless valuable in determining the target capital structure for the company in question.

Review the explicit or implicit goals and strategies management has for the company. This will reveal how the capital structure should develop over time. For example, if management is planning acquisitions, it is likely that debt will grow significantly in order to finance the acquisitions. As mentioned, management tries to balance operative risk against financial risk. Therefore, one can conclude that a riskier strategy will probably result in a less aggressive capital structure (i.e. less debt).

Finally, as yet another reference point in determining the target capital structure, calculate the debt/equity ratio that will provide the lowest possible WACC, subject to a satisfactory interest coverage and operative/financial risk ratio. The interest coverage, i.e. the amount of earnings available for interest payments, should be of such magnitude

Interest coverage equals the amount of earnings available for interest payments, i.e. EBIT/(interest expense + required preferred dividends)

as to give sufficient margin in case of a downturn or external shock. For example, in order for company debt to be classified by credit rating agencies as 'investment grade', one demand is that the interest coverage needs to be over 2. Of course, the closer the interest coverage is to 1, the higher the risk of defaulting on the interest payments. The interest coverage is consequently a measure of financial risk where a lower coverage represents a higher risk. This risk should be balanced against the operative risk. For example, a high-growth biotechnology company with volatile cash flows should generally have higher interest coverage than a mature industrial company with stable historical and projected future cash flows.

Based on the above four ways of analyzing the capital structure, you should be able to decide a reasonable target capital structure for the company in question.

Cost of capital – equity financing

The cost of equity, or the required return on shareholders' equity, is the cost at which a company can attract additional money from external investors. In other words, it is the return investors require in order to invest in the company instead of somewhere else. As such, it may be regarded as the opportunity cost for the equity provider. The cost of equity comprises two components – the risk-free interest that investors earn on a risk-free investment and an additional yield that is appropriate for the level of risk that the investor takes when investing in the company. There are several ways of calculating the cost of equity, but the most common and best-known approach is the so-called capital asset pricing model (CAPM). The following formula shows how the cost of equity is calculated using CAPM:

CAPM: cost of equity = risk-free rate of return + (market risk premium × beta)

■ The risk-free rate of return usually refers to the return on a government bond or a treasury bill in the home country of the company being valued with a duration that matches the investor's investment horizon. As an equity investment is usually a relatively long-term investment, a bond with a longer duration should be used. We recommend the use of a 10- to 15-year government bond since the liquidity of bonds with very long durations, for example 30 years, is usually limited.

▪ The market risk premium is the average risk premium that is required to invest in a risky security (for example, shares) compared with 'safe' investments (for example, government bonds). Historically, this risk premium has hovered between 2.5 and 4.5 per cent for traded companies but it needs to be adjusted, depending on the market. Yearly research is conducted on the risk premium in a number of different markets so updated localized figures can be found.

▪ Beta is a measure of the systematic or company-specific risk that is associated with a company. A beta greater than 1 means that the company is judged to have a higher risk and return than the market in general while a beta below 1 means that the company has a lower risk and return than the market in general. If the company to be valued is not publicly traded, it is usually difficult to determine or estimate beta. In such cases, a solution might be to use a beta for a comparable company with similar characteristics or, if available, a beta for the relevant sector.

Cost of capital – non-equity financing

The cost of capital for non-equity financing or the required return on debt is the cost to the company of attracting more money from external lenders, in the first instance banks and other lending institutions. This refers to the interest that the lender requires to lend its money to the company. Note that the cost of capital is calculated on the market value of debts and not through dividing the interest expense on the profit and loss account by the liabilities on the balance sheet. Instead, the cost of capital for non-equity capital can be calculated using the following formula:

Cost for non-equity finance capital = risk-free rate of return + reasonable risk premium

If the company recently borrowed money, the interest on that loan is generally a good indication of the cost of debt. If there are no such recent transactions for the company in question, look for transactions with similar companies in the same industry and use that interest rate as the cost of non-equity finance for the company that is to be valued.

Clearly, it is relatively simple to calculate the cost of capital on debt. The above formula requires, however, that the debt is fairly standardized. Other calculation methods should be used if the structure is more complicated, for example if the company uses complex interest structures, foreign loans, convertible debentures, mezzanine financing, etc. These involve calculations that fall outside the scope of this book and instead we refer interested readers to the Further reading section at the end of this book.

Another way of estimating cost of equity – CAPM vs ECE

As mentioned, CAPM is a theoretically correct method of calculating the cost of equity. However, it is rather complicated to calculate and it may be difficult to derive, for example for smaller or unlisted companies. This is because a CAPM computation requires information on the market value of equity and beta, numbers that are not easily available for unlisted companies.

The first shortcut to use when valuing this kind of company is to 'borrow' numbers from similar companies traded on the public market. By using their beta, we can achieve an acceptable approximation.

The second shortcut at hand, if the necessary data are simply not available, is to estimate the cost of equity capital, sometimes referred to as ECE (estimated cost of equity). The ECE is derived from four variables:

1 The general market discount rate for stocks.
2 Discount rates for companies in the same industry.
3 Discount rates for companies at the same stage.
4 The level of risk specific for this company, i.e. the riskiness of the future cash flows.

In this way, we may indirectly estimate an appropriate cost of equity instead of calculating it via the CAPM formula.

When estimating the equity discount rate, the market discount rate can be used as a starting point. Calculate this using the following formula:

Market discount rate = risk-free rate + market risk premium

The risk-free rate is the interest rate that one earns from a risk-free investment over a given period. Usually, this is the interest payable on an interest-bearing security issued by the government with a term equal to the investment period. A 10-year government bond is generally recommended. The interest on such a security currently (June 2010) stands at 3.8 per cent in Euroland and 3.3 per cent in the US.

The market risk premium is the premium that the average investor requires to invest in an average share on the market. Clearly, a share carries a greater risk than a risk-free investment and consequently the average investor demands a higher return to compensate for the higher risk. In Europe, where the market risk premium over the past 10 years has been between 2.5 and 4.5 per cent (Damodoran, December 2009), the market's cost of capital, the market discount rate, which reflects the risk of investing in the stock market in general, has been between 6 and 8 per cent.

As a second parameter, check the discount rates of comparable companies. How do investment bank analysts assess their risk? How do those companies differ from the one you are about to value? If the risk is higher, the discount rate should correspondingly also be higher.

If we start at one end of the cost of capital spectrum, let us assume a risk-free rate around 3.5 per cent. This represents the lower extreme regarding cost of capital. At the other extreme we have small, high-growth and early-stage companies, where the risk is evidently much higher than for a risk-free investment or compared with mature companies with stable cash flows. So at the other extreme there are, for example, venture capital firms that invest in early-stage companies, where the demanded return on equity often lies somewhere between 30 and 70 per cent depending on when in the company's lifecycle the investment is made. Often these companies may not have any debt at all, as banks will not lend to them due to the lack of cash flows, the cost of capital is the same as the cost of equity. You can safely assume that the cost of equity capital lies between these extremes.

So, for a hypothetical company, we could have the following reference points to work with in estimating the cost of capital:

Risk-free rate of return	General demanded return for a stock market investment	Average for a group of comparable companies	The most comparable company in sector	Demanded return on equity for venture capital in the sector
3.5%	7%	15%	18%	40%

Finally, you need to do the usual WACC calculation based on the ECE you have decided for the equity. If the company has no debt, which is more common in the case of younger companies, the estimated cost of equity becomes the WACC since the debt-related part of the equation equals zero.

In order to estimate the company-specific risk, it is necessary to analyze its fundamental business activities and the factors critical for the company's success. These factors are identical to the company's value drivers, which are fundamental to predicting future cash flows. In Chapter 7, 'Underlying analysis and key value drivers', we present a model for analyzing the company's activities, its environment and its key value drivers.

When using ECE, it could be useful to perform a sensitivity analysis in order to check that the valuation is reasonable. This involves, for example, valuing the company using both the lowest reasonable discount rate you believe the company could have and also the highest. The result is a range within which the company's value probably lies.

Calculating free cash flow

Calculating free cash flow means calculating the cash flows to which all the company's claimants have access and which will be used to reimburse all capital providers to the company. Note the difference between the company's reported profits and free cash flows. The reported profit includes a number of entries, such as depreciation, transfers to accruals funds or other tax-free reserves that do not affect the company's cash flows. The difference between the company's reported profit and its cash flows is often considerable.

> Calculating free cash flow means calculating the cash flows to which all the company's claimants have access

When calculating free cash flows, it is common to divide the company's future into two periods – the explicit forecast period and the terminal value period, also known as the implicit forecast period. During the explicit forecast period, which comprises the small number of years for which it is possible to predict cash flows with reasonable accuracy, free cash flows are calculated for each individual year. For the terminal value period, it is difficult and time-consuming to predict free cash flows year by year since it means predicting what will happen during a period stretching far into the future. Instead, one usually calculates a terminal value, which is a value equivalent to all the discounted free cash flows from the first year after the explicit period until infinity. The calculation of enterprise value can consequently be expressed as:

Enterprise value = present value of cash flow during explicit forecast period
+ present value of cash flow after explicit period
(terminal value period)

The length of the explicit period varies depending on company, industry and situation. In the terminal value period, one uses the same growth figure for all years and hence we must assume that growth will be constant throughout that period. Therefore, the explicit forecast period must last until the year after which growth can be assumed to be constant. For example, if growth is assumed to be irregular until the end of year six, the explicit forecast period will cover years one to six.

Another limit to how long the explicit period needs to be is the level of growth we estimate for the company. As long as the growth is higher than the WACC, the calculations need to be explicit. This means that if you assume that the company that you are valuing will experience growth of 15 per cent during years seven to 12 and the cost of capital will be 12 per cent, then the cash flows of these years need to be treated explicitly and cannot be included in the terminal value calculation. However, calculating free cash flow for a specific year is likely to become more inaccurate the further into the future it lies, so an explicit forecast period longer than 10 years is seldom recommended. Instead, with companies experiencing high growth for many years, the valuation can be divided into three periods, something we will return to later.

The terminal value period begins when the company's growth can be assumed to be constant at approximately the level of general gross domestic product (GDP) growth; this last phase of a company's growth development is often referred to as the steady-state period. When this period begins varies significantly depending on company and industry; for certain companies it may begin after three years, for others after eight years and for yet others after 15 years. There is no standard guideline.

When calculating free cash flows for every individual year, you start with the current year and use data in the income statement and balance sheet. Thereafter you need to rework the accounting data to 'real' data, i.e. data that correspond to the company's cash flow.

Calculate free cash flow for a given year in the following way:

```
+ Earnings before interest and taxes (EBIT)
− cash taxes on EBIT
− investments
+ depreciation
+/− change in working capital
= free cash flow
```

In other words, in order to calculate free cash flow, the following five variables are required:

1 earnings before interest and taxes (EBIT)

2 cash taxes on EBIT

3 investments

4 depreciation

5 change in working capital.

The following presumes that you have forecasted income statements and balance sheets for the relevant years. The first variable that we need is EBIT, which is an item to be taken straight off the income statement of the company and thus does not have to be calculated or analyzed.

The second variable is the cash taxes on EBIT which are computed as follows in the McKinsey model:

> + Tax on profit and loss account
> + tax deductible from interest payments (calculated as interest payments ×
>   company tax rate)
> – tax on interest income (calculated as interest income × company tax rate)
> – tax on non-operating income
> = taxes on EBIT

Note that taxes on EBIT are often higher than the taxes that appear on the profit and loss account. This is because taxes on EBIT are not affected by the financing structure. The tax shield that many companies enjoy due to their liabilities should not affect taxes on EBIT. In the McKinsey model, the tax shield is treated in the calculation of the WACC instead (see previous section). The WACC is adjusted downwards and thereby increases both the discounted cash flow and company value.

The third variable is investments, which simply refers to investments in inventory, machines and the like that are deemed to fall in the current year and which therefore affect this year's cash flow. If investments are not accounted for separately, they can be derived from the net change in fixed assets between this year's balance sheets and the previous after adding the depreciation on the assets.

If the company has made investments, it will also have depreciation charges. Depreciation is an accounting technique used to spread the cost of investments over the economic lifetime of an asset reducing the year's results in line with the wear and tear of the investment. The cash flow, however, is only affected when an investment is paid for and is consequently unaltered by depreciation. This is true for all types of depreciation, including depreciation of goodwill. When depreciation is incorporated into the measure of earnings being used, EBIT, all depreciation must be reapplied to the earnings. The cash effects of depreciation are accounted for in the tax calculation.

The fifth and final variable is the change in working capital. Working capital refers to capital tied up in liquid cash, customer credits, inventory, the net between customer accounts and suppliers' debt and other interest-free debts. As a company grows, working capital often increases too, which reduces cash flow and thus value. Changes in working capital affect the free cash flow from year to year and are calculated as follows:

Increase (–)/decrease (+) in liquid cash
Increase (–)/decrease (+) in customer accounts
Increase (–)/decrease (+) in inventory
Increase (+)/decrease (–) in suppliers' debts
Increase (+)/decrease (–) in other non-interest-bearing operating debts
= +/– Changes in working capital

Skilled working capital management increases cash flow and thereby value

This calculation of the change in working capital is performed for each year in the explicit forecast period. An increase in working capital reduces free cash flow, and a decrease in working capital increases the free cash flow. Therefore, skilled working capital management is often an important value-creation opportunity that should not be overlooked.

Finally, when you have calculated the free cash flows year by year, you will need to discount them one by one back to today using the following formula:

Value today of FCF from the explicit period

$$= FCF = \frac{FCF_1}{(1 + WACC)^1} + \frac{FCF_2}{(1 + WACC)^2} + ... \frac{FCF_t}{(1 + WACC)^t}$$

where FCF_1 is the cash flow year 1 and FCF_t is the cash flow t years into the future, WACC is the weighted average cost of capital and t is the number of years in the explicit period.

You now have the enterprise value stemming from the explicit period. In order to get the enterprise value, you need to add the present value of all free cash flows after the explicit period to infinity (i.e. the terminal value).

Computing terminal value

Having calculated the free cash flow for the explicit forecast period, we move on to calculate the free cash flows from the year after the last year of the explicit period to perpetuity. This value, discounted back to today, is referred to as the 'terminal value' or 'continuing value'.

As this calculation stretches far into the future, it is difficult to be accurate. However, the calculation is of the utmost importance since the lion's share of a company's value is often derived from the terminal forecast period. It is not unusual for as much as 70–80 per cent of a company's value to stem from this period.

Terminal value often constitutes the majority of total enterprise value

Note that it is theoretically possible to use a long explicit forecast period instead of the terminal value technique. The explicit forecast period could then be extended to, for example, 50 years, and the free cash flow is calculated for each year. In this way, the value of the free cash flow after the explicit forecast period (i.e. after 50 years) becomes so small it may be disregarded. However, there are obvious difficulties with doing exact and explicit forecasts so far into the future. Therefore, the terminal value technique that implicitly accounts for all free cash flows for the period from the first year of steady state until infinity is generally preferred.

The terminal value calculations are conducted through the following three steps:

1 Estimate a constant growth from the first year in the terminal value period until infinity.
2 Take the estimated free cash flow for the last year of the explicit forecast period, and multiply it by the constant growth factor $(1 + g)$.
3 Discount using the appropriate discount rate less the constant growth.

Expressed as a formula, terminal value is calculated as:

$$TV = \frac{FCF_{t+1}}{WACC - g}$$

where FCF_{t+1} equals the level of free cash flow in the first year after the explicit forecast period, t is the number of years in the explicit period, WACC equals the weighted average cost of capital and g is the expected growth rate in free cash flow in perpetuity.

Note that it is very important to determine the year in which the free cash flow begins to grow at a constant rate, i.e. which year's cash flow will be used in the above formula. This is because the entire terminal value calculation (and thus a significant portion of the company's value) is based on the cash flow from the last explicit year.

Another variable with great value impact is the rate at which the constant growth is set. It has an enormous effect on the terminal value and consequently on the total company valuation. In the long run, industry growth cannot exceed GDP growth as it would mean that the industry would equal the GDP. For example, in Euroland, the inflation target is between 1 and 2 per cent and real GDP growth has been 3.46 per cent between 1980 and 2009 (source: International Monetary Fund), which means that long-term nominal growth for many companies is likely to hover between 4.5 and 5.5 per cent. The long-term growth for different industries varies but it is hard to motivate a number that is much higher than that of general GDP.

The formula above gives a terminal value at year t, the last year of the explicit forecast period, not a value today. In order to come to the final terminal value today, in other words the value today of all the free cash flows following the explicit forecast period, this value must be discounted back from the end of the explicit period until today using the discount rate. This is expressed as the formula:

$$TV_0 = \frac{TV_1}{(1 + WACC)^t}$$

This value is the so-called terminal value and corresponds to today's value of all free cash flows following the explicit forecast period until infinity.

A third period for companies experiencing hypergrowth

As mentioned earlier, the classic DCF model requires the estimation of the discounted cash flows in two periods – the explicit and the terminal value period. For many high-growth companies this division into two periods is less than ideal for several reasons. Firstly, there is the problem that the growth rate must be constant for the terminal value period. This might involve having to move directly from an extremely high growth rate to the much lower steady-state growth. This rarely reflects the reality of the high-growth company as it may experience extreme growth for several years, then a period of higher than long-term growth for another few years and finally a period during which growth is constant at a given long-term growth rate. Consequently, the estimations can instead be divided into three periods.

When using a third, middle period, the explicit value period is, as long as it is fruitful to do the calculations explicitly, subject to accuracy and control. Then follows a period of higher than long-term growth covering the period during which the growth is higher than the estimated cost of capital. During this period, sometimes called the hypergrowth period, the high-growth company is assumed to experience constant growth at a rate that is higher than the long-term growth. This period should be as long as it is reasonable to assume that the company will experience this higher growth rate. The following formula applies:

Value today of FCF from the hypergrowth period

$$= FCF_0 = \frac{FCF_t \times g_{t+1}}{(1 + WACC)^{t+1}} + \frac{FCF_{t+2} \times g_{t+2}}{(1 + WACC)^{t+2}} + \ldots + \frac{FCF_{t+2} \times g_{t+z}}{(1 + WACC)^{t+z}}$$

where FCF_t is the free cash flow of the last year of the explicit period, t is the number of years of the explicit period, g is the level of growth for the year in question, WACC is the weighted average cost of capital and z is the number of years in the hypergrowth period.

Starting with the year that the company achieves its long-term growth rate, calculate the terminal value period using the method described above. Note that the cash flow that is used to calculate the terminal value period is the cash flow for the last year of the hypergrowth period rather than the cash flow during the last year of the explicit value period.

Discounting and final corporate value

Finally, all the discounted free cash flows from the explicit value period, a possible hypergrowth period and the terminal value period are added together in order to calculate the total present value of all future free cash flows. Moreover, after having been discounted back to today, all other non-operating cash flows are also added, as shown in Figure 6.2.

1

Explicit period (g>WACC) – each year's cash flow calculated and discounted separately

Value today of FCF from the explicit period = $FCF_0 = FCF_1/(1+WACC) + FCF_2/(1+WACC)^2 + ... + FCF_t/(1+WACC)^t$

Where FCF_0 is the free cash flow value today (year 0), FCF_t is the cash flow t years into the future and WACC is the weighted average cost of capital.

2

Hypergrowth period (g>WACC>long-term g) – the cash flow of the last year of the explicit period is used as a base. A year-by-year calculation is done based solely on this cash flow with the appropriate level of growth (which may vary from year to year). All cash flows are discounted back to today (period 0).

Value today of FCF from the hypergrowth period = $(FCF_t \times (1+g))/(1+WACC)^{t+1} + (FCF_t \times (1+g)^2)/(1+WACC)^{t+2} + ...$
$+ (FCF_t \times (1+g)^z)/(1+WACC)^{t+z}$

Where FCF_t is the free cash flow of the last year of the explicit period, t is the number of years of the explicit period, g is the level of growth for the year in question, WACC is the weighted average cost of capital and z is the number of years in the hypergrowth period.

3

Terminal value (WACC>g)
1. The value of all cash flows from the year after the last year of the hypergrowth period to infinity.
2. The value from step 1 is then discounted back to today.

1. $TV_{t+z} = FCF_{t+z+1}/(WACC - g)$
2. $TV_0 = TV_{t+z}/(1 + WACC)^{t+z}$

Where FCF_{t+z+1} equals the level of free cash flow in the first year after the hypergrowth period, t+z is the number of years in the explicit plus hypergrowth periods, WACC equals the weighted average cost of capital and g is the expected growth rate in free cash flow in perpetuity.

FIGURE 6.2 How to add up the three periods

This can also be expressed as follows:

> \+ The sum of all discounted free cash flows for the explicit value period
> \+ The discounted value of the hypergrowth period (if you have decided on this method)
> \+ The discounted terminal value
> +/– Non-operating discounted free cash flows
> \= Total discounted free cash flow = value of the company's assets = enterprise value

Value per share equals value of equity/ number of shares in the company

The total discounted cash flow comprises the present value of future cash flows derived from the company's total assets. As the company valuation is usually conducted in order to calculate the value of the shareholders' equity, i.e. the value that belongs to the shareholders (which is what is bought and sold via the company's shares), the market value of the company's debts is subtracted from the present value that has been calculated.

> Total discounted free cash flows (= enterprise value)
> – market value of interest-bearing debts
> \+ non-operating assets
> \= equity value = value of the company for its shareholders

In order to derive the value per share, the shareholders' equity is divided by the number of shares.

$$\text{Value per share} = \frac{\text{market value of equity}}{\text{number of shares in the company}}$$

The value provided by a DCF valuation is the theoretical market value of the company based on the assumptions and forecasts made

We have now completed a full DCF valuation including all the steps specified at the beginning of the chapter. The value provided is the theoretical market value of a company and its shares based on the assumptions and forecasts made.

The most important variables in a DCF analysis

You might ask which input variables are critical and which you should concentrate on when preparing to conduct a DCF valuation. Previously we mentioned five variables that affect free cash flows:

1 investments

2 taxes

3 depreciation

4 changes in working capital

5 EBIT.

Of these, EBIT has the greatest impact on value for most companies. An analysis of EBIT is essentially concerned with an analysis of the company's revenues. This is because trends relating to the company's costs are generally easier to predict than its revenues. Costs are often more under the control of the management than revenues since revenues are more affected by external factors. Therefore, costs are generally forecasted more correctly. Consequently, revenue trends and forecasted growth/decline in revenues is the single most important variable when future cash flow is being predicted.

Since it is not abnormal that the majority of a company's value stems from the terminal value period, it is particularly important to analyze long-term revenue trends.

Apart from revenue prediction, four areas should receive extra attention:

1 The historical relationship between revenues and changes in working capital and estimates of how this will evolve in the future.

2 EBIT for the last year of the explicit value period.

3 The growth in EBIT for the terminal value period.

4 The cost of capital. Ensure that it corresponds to the inherent risk in the predicted cash flows.

Table 6.2 shows how changes in these critical parameters (all other variables held constant) affect the value of a hypothetical company. From Table 6.2 we see that even small changes in the above-mentioned variables have a major effect on the value of the company. In other words, it is of the utmost importance to estimate these variables as correctly as possible. In turn, these variables are determined by the company's underlying operations and the strengths, weaknesses, opportunities and threats that face it.

Table 6.2: Critical variables and their effect on terminal value

	WACC (%)	FCF_t	FCF_g (%)	Terminal value	% of base case value
Base scenario	15	40,822	5	408,220	100
Scenario 1	15	45,000	5	450,000	110
Scenario 2	15	35,000	5	350,000	86
Scenario 3	20	40,822	5	272,147	67
Scenario 4	10	40,822	5	816,440	200
Scenario 5	15	40,822	10	816,440	200
Scenario 6	15	40,822	3	340,183	83

FCF_t is free cash flow in the last year of the explicit period, FCF_g is the growth rate in the free cash flow in perpetuity, WACC is the weighted average cost of capital.

The DCF approach – only a calculation machine

As mentioned earlier, the McKinsey model, as well as all other valuation models, is nothing more than a calculation machine, and the value that emerges from the model is completely dependent on the value it has been fed with. What does this mean? It is tempting to believe that provided there are no computing errors or technical problems, the model always gives a more or less correct company valuation. The reality is that the model can produce any value at all even if applied correctly. The value is completely dependent on how the input variables are estimated and handled. The model itself merely transforms the basic input variables into a value in accordance with the model.

Consequently, as long as the valuation model is correct, it is only of secondary importance to the valuation. Rather, it is the underlying analysis that decides the input variables for the model resulting in the greatest impact on the value, and therefore this deserves the most time and attention.

Checking your assumptions

In order to double-check your DCF valuation, we recommend using fundamental and relative multiples as well. This is because all valuation models are mathematically interconnected and will give rise to the same results,[1] given the same underlying assumptions. This may sound like a rather revolutionary concept, but it is old news in the academic world.[2] Despite this, it is still very useful.

This fact has immense practical implications. The two most important are:

1 The differences between the various valuation models are not that they yield different results but that each model highlights certain aspects while omitting others. With the knowledge that all models are interconnected, you can check what your assumptions from one model mean expressed as assumptions in another. For example, given certain DCF assumptions, we can express this in a long-term return on equity (ROE) or long-term P/E ratio and check whether what we thought to be reasonable DCF assumptions are still reasonable expressed in other terms.

2 An end to confusing and contradictory valuation estimates, for example equity that is cheap according to P/E but expensive according to a DCF valuation. With a method for making assumptions coherent, all models will yield approximately the same results. This, it is hoped, will produce a healthy shift in all valuation discussions from model technicalities to the underlying assumptions.

As a consequence, the choice of valuation model is really one of taste and preference. Most models basically aim to calculate the net present value of future cash flows and they all need to deal with how to find the proper discount rate.

In order for this translation process to be acceptably manageable, the following simplifying assumptions have to be made:

1 All value is derived from the terminal value period.

2 Clean surplus requirements hold. Basically, the clean surplus requirement means that growth in the capital stock equals new investment and growth in book value equals growth in retained earnings plus new equity issues.

3 No new equity issues.

---

[1] For the mathematical proofs, see, for example, 'On the general equivalence of company valuation models', pp. 235–333 in *Essays in Company Valuation*, Joakim Levin, Stockholm, EFI, 1998.

[2] F. Modigliani and M. Miller made this observation in 1961 in the article 'Dividend policy, growth and the valuation of shares' in the *Journal of Business* (see Further reading).

4 All growth rates and ratios remain constant during the long-term sustainable equilibrium.

5 No increase in holdings of cash and marketable securities. This basically means that companies are assumed not to accumulate cash, but instead pay dividends or equivalent.

6 Marginal return on capital equals average return on capital during the long-term equilibrium.

7 The debt to equity ratio is constant. Debt consequently grows at the same speed as accumulated earnings increase the equity.

8 Interest rates are constant and therefore the value of debt is constant (except for the above change as equity grows).

9 Minorities are ignored.

If the above nine assumptions hold, it is possible to interpret any of the most popular valuation approaches into a number of implied assumptions from another valuation approach. These calculations will of course not yield exact results but may be regarded as an extra input in your reality check of your DCF valuation. A full analysis and mathematical explanations of this exercise fall outside the scope of this book and we refer the interested reader to the Further reading section at the end of this book.

Table 6.3 is a guide on how to transform DCF data to other implied key financial measures that can be used to check your underlying assumptions. In Chapter 8 we will show how to use this guide in practice.

Table 6.3: Formulas for translating DCF input data to other key financial measures

Data item	Symbol	Formula	Example
Data required for DCF			
Free cash flow	FCF		10
Free cash flow growth	g		5%
WACC	WACC	$(E/(D+E)) \times C_E + (D/(D+E)) \times C_D(1-T)$	6%
Tax rate	T		30%
Cost of equity	C_E		8%
Cost of debt	C_D		6%
New investments	Invest		30

Table 6.3 *Continued*

Data item	Symbol	Formula	Example
Value of debt/enterprise value	D/(D+E)		50%
Implied data for DCF			
Enterprise value	EV	FCF/(WACC–g)	1,000
Value of debt	D	EV×(D/(E+D))	500
Value of equity	E	EV–D	500
Free cash flow yield		WACC–g	1%
Implied data for return on capital model			
Net operating profit after tax	NOPAT	FCF+Invest	40
Return on capital	ROC	NOPAT×g/Invest×100	6.7%
Capital	K	NOPAT/ROC×100	600
Cost of capital		WACC	6%
Return on capital spread		(ROC–WACC)	0.7%
Value added	VA	(ROC–WACC)×K	4
Present value of value added	PV (VA)	VA/(WACC–g)	400
Enterprise value to capital ratio		(K+PV(VA))/K	1.7
Implied data for dividend discount model			
Interest payments (after tax)	INT	D×C_D×(1–T)	21
New debt finance	ND	D×g	25
Dividends	Div	FCF+ND–INT	14
Earnings	Earn	Div+Invest–ND	19

Data item	Symbol	Formula	Example
Payout ratio	p	Div/Earn	73.68%
Dividend yield	DivY	$C_E - g$	3%
Price/earnings ratio	P/Earn	$p/(C_E - g)$	24.6
Implied data for dynamic ROE model			
Return on equity	ROE	$g/(1-p)$	19%
Cost of equity	C_E		8%
ROE spread		$ROE - C_E$	11%
Equilibrium book value	BV	Earn/ROE	100
Value added	VA	$(ROE - C_E) \times BV$	11
Present value of value added		$VA/(C_E - g)$	367
Price to book value	P/BV	$P/Earn \times ROE$	4.67

Summary

In this chapter, we have presented the so-called McKinsey version of the most commonly used valuation model, the discounted cash flow model. A valuation according to this model covers the following key steps:

- **Estimating the cost of capital**: the most commonly used cost of capital approach is the weighted average cost of capital (WACC). The WACC computation includes estimating the cost of debt, the cost of equity and the target capital structure. We also presented an alternative way to estimate the cost of capital directly by using a number of references.

- **Estimating free cash flow in the explicit period**, by forecasting earnings before interest and tax (EBIT), taxes, investments, depreciations and changes in working capital and discounting each year's free cash flow back to today. The explicit period should be extended to cover every year up to the so-called steady state where growth can be assumed to be constant.

- **Estimating terminal period value**, i.e. from the first year after the explicit period to perpetuity, by determining free cash flow for the last year of the explicit period, growth in free cash flow to infinity and cost of capital and discount it back to today. We noted that it is not uncommon for a majority of the value of the company to derive from the terminal value.

■ **Add up all values**, i.e. the terminal value, the value from the explicit period, the value from a possible hypergrowth period and any non-operational free cash flow to arrive at the total enterprise value. In order to get the value of the company's equity, we subtracted the market value of debt and other claims such as pension provisions and minority interests.

For certain companies that do not reach a steady-state growth for a long time, it can be beneficial to use a third period, called the hypergrowth period, between the explicit period and the terminal value period.

Furthermore, we noted that a DCF model is nothing more than a calculator and you can obtain whatever result you wish by manipulating the inputs. Therefore, the underlying analysis where the input variables are determined is of utmost importance.

Finally, we presented a way to test your DCF assumptions by analyzing what these assumptions imply in terms of financial ratios, such as return on capital (ROC), return on equity (ROE) or P/E. This exercise is possible since under certain assumptions, most valuation models are in fact coherent and will produce the same results.

The next chapter describes the underlying analysis in more detail as well as the concept of value drivers.

7

Underlying analysis and key value drivers

What topics are covered in this chapter?

- What is a value driver?
- How to identify key value drivers
- Structuring the underlying analysis
- Generic operational value drivers
- Framework for the underlying analysis
- Temporary monopolies – an additional tool for the underlying analysis
- Summary

In this chapter, we will be taking a closer look at the so-called underlying analysis and key value drivers.

As stated in the previous chapter, the result of a DCF valuation is entirely dependent on the data entered into the model. These inputs are the result of an analysis of:

- the macroeconomic situation
- the industry structure and trends
- the company strengths and weaknesses and key economic and financial variables

▪ the corporate strategy

▪ all other information that substantially affects future cash flows of the company.

This analysis of the company's business and its environment is crucial for the quality of the valuation. Certainly, you need to master the DCF calculation 'machine' but once you know the technique, your focus should shift to the value creation process of the company (see Figure 7.1).

When analyzing a company's business, all variables affecting the company value should be considered. However, this is an extensive exercise and will cover a great number of variables, which makes the analysis very

In order to make the analysis easier to implement, the analysis is usually focused on a definite number of so-called value drivers

difficult to work through and use. Furthermore, there are obvious difficulties in structuring an analysis with hundreds of variables, because it is complex and multifaceted. In order to make the analysis easier to implement, the analysis is usually focused on a definite number of so-called value drivers.

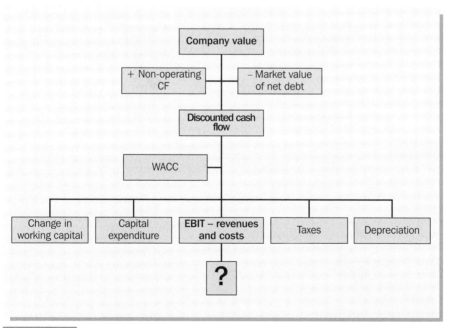

FIGURE 7.1   Relationship between the DCF model and the underlying analysis

What is a value driver?

In order to understand value creation in a company, you need to locate and understand where the value is created, which means identifying the so-called value drivers of the business. A thorough understanding of the value drivers and their effect on the company's future cash flow will help you to estimate the input variables in the DCF model.

In order to understand how value is created you need to identify the so-called value drivers

Understanding the key value drivers is one of management's most important tasks since it is clearly difficult to maximize value without knowing where it is created

Normally there are hundreds of value drivers, each adding a fraction of value to the total enterprise value (for examples of these, see the value driver list in Appendix A). When doing a valuation, determining, analyzing and understanding all these value drivers is usually not possible. Instead, you want to focus your efforts on the value drivers that add most to overall company value. These are characteristically referred to as 'key value drivers'. The value drivers that are key value drivers vary from company to company and from industry to industry. Consequently, the value impact of the key value drivers also varies.

One needs to distinguish between financial value drivers such as operating margins or return on invested capital (ROIC) and non-financial or operating value drivers.

Financial value drivers

Value drivers exist at all levels within an organization. At top management level, a key value driver usually reflects the overall performance of the entire company. Therefore, they are more often in the form of financial value drivers and they tend to be generic from business unit to business unit, from company to company and from industry to industry. Typical financial key value drivers are return on invested capital (ROIC), return on equity (ROE), operating margins, revenue growth and working capital changes.

Operating value drivers

A difference between financial and operative value drivers is that the former measures the company's performance for a certain period in the past. Operational value drivers, on the other hand, can function as early indicators of the company's future performance and hence future cash flow. For example, increased customer churn indicates a coming drop in sales, while increased sales of newly developed products indicate that the company's product portfolio will be competitive in the future.

How to identify key value drivers

Identifying the key value drivers within a company is usually not a simple task since it presupposes an understanding of the overall value creation process in the company. In addition, key value drivers are not static, but might change from time to time and a periodic review of the analysis is needed. As the financial key value drivers are more or less generic, it is advisable to start the analysis by determining them for the entire company and for key business units and/or subsidiaries. With the financial key value drivers in place, one needs to analyze the effects on the financial key value drivers of changes in various operational variables in the company as well as in its environment in order to find key operational value drivers. Here, scenario analysis is recommended not only to review the effect of changes in the potential key value drivers, but also to understand how they relate to each other.

It can be of great help to review industry structure and/or intellectual capital literature in order to understand how these relate to corporate value. A brief presentation of these two areas follows in the next section.

Structuring the underlying analysis

Our approach is to divide the underlying analysis into three parts: an external part, an internal part and the company's strategy as the link between the two, as shown in Figure 7.2 and as follows:

■ The external part consists of a macroeconomic analysis of the overall economic factors that affect the company, and an industry analysis of the industrial structure in which the company operates. We do not believe it is necessary to conduct a separate macroeconomic analysis and recommend instead focusing the external analysis on the industry structure analysis. The primary reason for this is that the macro-factor of greatest importance, economic growth and its effect on the industry, is already included in the industry growth variable. Secondly, it is very difficult to forecast macro-variables with sufficient precision to be of value in a company valuation.

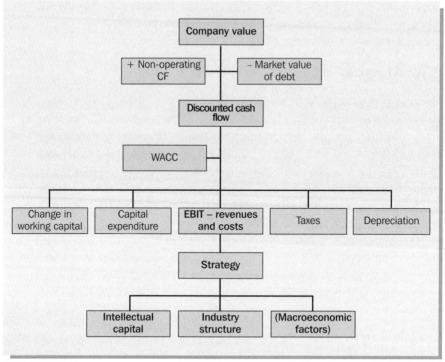

FIGURE 7.2   Structure for the underlying analysis

■ The company's internal resources, popularly known as its intellectual capital, comprise all the company's intangible resources, for example the knowledge of the employees, intellectual property and documented work processes through which the company controls its business.

■ The third part in the analysis is assessing the corporate strategy. The strategy is largely the way in which the management will achieve the corporate goals given its internal and external preconditions. The strategy itself does not contain any value drivers. Instead, the strategy deals with how the company exploits and extracts leverage from the key value drivers in the industry structure and from its intellectual capital. In this way, a chosen strategy can both increase and decrease the importance of a certain value driver.

Before we present the most common non-financial value drivers in more detail, we will describe the areas of industry structure and intellectual capital in more depth. We base this description on a well-known model in each respective area. For the analysis of industry structure, we will use Harvard professor Michael Porter's 'five forces' model.[1] For the analysis of intellectual capital we will use a model called 'the intellectual capital value tree', created by Leif Edvinsson, a pioneer in the area of intellectual capital.[2]

Industry structure

Industry analysis is always an important part of a valuation in order to be able to make the necessary assumptions. Porter's model analyzes the competitive structure of an industry based on what is called the five forces. The combined power of these five forces decides the potential for profit in the industry. Porter's five forces model is often presented as shown in Figure 7.3 and the five forces can be described as follows.

Rivalry

In general, it is true that the higher the rivalry in an industry, the lower the profitability

Companies in an industry are mutually dependent. This means that a competitive move from one company will have an effect on the others and, therefore, provoke a countermove. For example, these moves could be price competition, advertising campaigns, product launches or increased customer service. Of course, rivalry works differently in different industries and is affected by a number of different factors, for example industrial growth or barriers to exit. In general, it is true that the higher the rivalry in an industry, the lower the profitability. The best scenario for a specific company (though usually not for its customers) is that rivalry is low, for example because of high growth in the industry or few existing competitors in the market.

Barriers to entry and to exit

Barriers to entry is the common way of referring to factors that make it more difficult and/or more expensive to establish a presence in an industry. There is often a distinction made between natural barriers to entry, such as economies of scale, strong brands, patents or capital needs, and unnatural barriers to entry, such as regulations, state monopolies and tariffs. The most advantageous situation for the profitability of an industry is generally when barriers to entry are high and barriers to exit low. This lays a foundation for high profits in a stable environment where the risk

[1] Porter, M.E., *Competitive Strategy – techniques for analyzing industries and competitors*, New York, The Free Press, 1980.
[2] Edvinsson, L. and Malone, M., *The Proven Way to Establish your Company's Real Value by Measuring its Hidden Brainpower*, London, Harper Business, 1997.

of price competition is low. In the worst scenario, barriers to entry are low and barriers to exit high. This means that many enter the industry in the good times and nobody leaves it when times are bad.

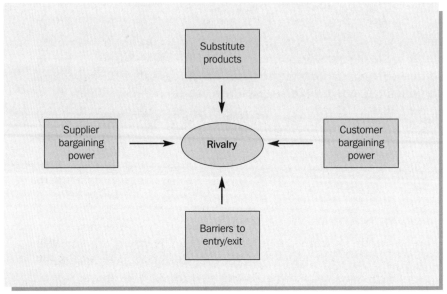

FIGURE 7.3   Porter's five forces model

Source: Adapted from Porter, M.E., *Competitive Strategy*, © 1980, 1998, The Free Press

Substitute products

A substitute is a product or service fulfilling the same need or function as the good or service in the industry under analysis. Substitute products limit profitability in an industry by setting an upper limit on the price of the product. A substitute to be particularly cautious about is a product or service that has been provided by an industry with high profits. At times of increased competition in that industry, prices will drop and these products will become a threat as a substitute.

Negotiating power of the suppliers

Suppliers can influence profitability in an industry if they have a strong position. They can, for example, raise prices, decrease the service level or take a number of other actions affecting the industry's structure. Examples of situations where the negotiating power of the supplier is high are:

▪ The supplier industry is dominated by a smaller number of companies and is more concentrated than the industry it sells to.

▪ The industry in question is not an important customer group for the supplier.

▪ The supplier constitutes a real threat to the industry through vertical integration. If the customers are not willing to pay higher prices, then the suppliers will begin to sell directly to the end consumer.

Negotiating power of the customer

Customers can influence the profitability in an industry in the same way by demanding lower prices, better service or better performance. Examples of factors that raise the negotiating power of the customers are:

▪ Customers are more concentrated than the sellers and buy in large volumes.

▪ Customers have low costs for changing supplier.

▪ The customers constitute a real threat to the suppliers through vertical integration, i.e. the buyers threaten the suppliers with producing the good or service themselves if the price does not go down.

With the aid of the above model, it is possible to analyze the industry in which your company is active. Does the industry have a high potential for profit? Is profitability going to be able to remain at the current level? The model is an excellent tool for analyzing the current and future situation for an industry.

Intellectual capital

Intellectual capital is sometimes defined as the difference between market value and the net asset value of a company. We consider this definition erroneous, not least when dealing with knowledge and high-growth companies. The net asset value has usually very little to do with market value and we do not believe it is possible to explain the difference between net asset value and market value using intellectual capital alone, as this necessitates excluding all macro-variables as well as the company's industry structure and strategy, all of which undeniably have an important influence on the market value. We believe a more correct definition to be: 'all non-financial assets of a company that are not reflected in the balance sheet'.

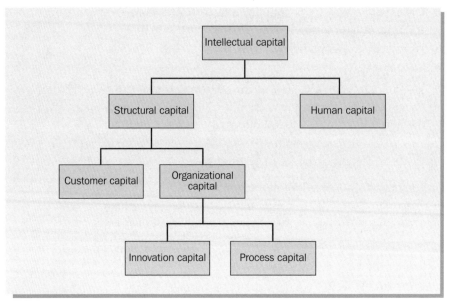

The intellectual capital value tree

To date, we lack an intellectual capital valuation model that can in a concrete fashion calculate the value of intellectual capital. However, this is also the case regarding the industry structure framework presented above and this framework has anyhow proven to be of immense use to valuation practitioners. To analyze a company's intellectual capital, we suggest the so-called intellectual capital value tree, presented in Figure 7.4. It was created by Leif Edvinsson and illustrates a way to structure the analysis of a company's intellectual capital.

Intellectual capital, according to this model, can be divided into human capital and structural capital. Human capital is the intellectual resources possessed by the individuals in the company and that leaves the company every evening when the employees leave the office. Structural capital is divided into two sub-groups: customer capital and organizational capital. Customer capital is defined as the value of all of the relationships the company has with its customers. Organizational capital consists of process and innovation capital. Process capital is all support systems, process documentation, manuals, IT systems and the like. Innovation capital consists mainly of brands, patents and documented ideas.

Generic operational value drivers

There are a large number of variables suitable for analysis in the areas of industry structure and intellectual capital that influence the value of a company. Sifting through all of these variables is time-consuming and to some extent unnecessary, which is the reason why most people who work with valuation choose a smaller number of variables to focus on.

In a study conducted at Stockholm School of Economics by the authors of this book in 1998, it was concluded that seven main non-financial value drivers seemed to have such general value impact that they verged on being generic. The Royal Swedish Academy of Engineering Sciences first published these findings in 1999 in 'Valuation of Growth Companies'.

Note that these variables can vary from company to company and from industry to industry

We will present and describe these seven variables and offer suggestions on how it is possible to measure them. It is important to note that these variables can vary from company to company and from industry to industry. When you analyze a company for valuation purposes, you should not take for granted that precisely these seven variables are the most suitable. If you find other variables with greater explanatory value, you should of course use them instead. However, in most cases, at least a few of the operational key value drivers can be found among these seven and serve as a basis for your analysis.

Industry structure value drivers

In the industry structure there are three key value drivers as outlined under the following headings.

Level of consolidation

The level of consolidation, i.e. the number of companies in an industry, is a measure of the competition. If an industry has 200 competing companies, it is possible to assume that competition is hard and margins low. If, on the other hand, there are only three companies in the industry, then one can expect higher margins and maybe even a certain measure of co-competition.

The more the company's position can be compared to a monopoly, the more attractive the company's position is. The reason for this is, of course, that a monopolist enjoys advantages that companies exposed to competition simply do not. The monopolist can set higher prices for its products and services or limit the supply if prices drop too low. Furthermore, the monopolist can fine-tune pricing based on the ability to set different prices for different customers and thus maximize profits. Finally, the monopolist can exercise low costs due to volume production and occupy a strong negotiating position with regard to the suppliers.

One way of measuring the level of consolidation is through the company's relative market share. This is done by dividing the company's market share by the sum of the market shares of, for example, the four biggest players in the industry. This measure gives a good indication of how dominant a company is in a specific industry as well as of the general level of competition in the industry.

Barriers to entry

As mentioned earlier in this chapter, there are two types of barrier to entry: natural and unnatural. Natural barriers to entry could be economies of scale, large start-up costs or strong brands. These can all result in a monopoly-like situation in an otherwise competitive market. Unnatural barriers to entry could be, for instance, regulations, state monopoly or similar interventions in the market limiting the number of existing competitors. As explained in the previous section, the level of competition in an industry is of the utmost importance for profitability. The level of consolidation gives a snapshot of what the industry looks like today, but gives no information on what it will look like in the future. The principal indicator of durability for a certain industry structure is its barriers to entry. When, for example, a certain company has achieved a monopoly-like position, it is the barriers to entry that will decide how long this position can be maintained. A monopoly-like situation without high barriers to entry will not last long, as other players will take notice and establish themselves on the market.

Barriers to entry can be measured in two currencies – time and money. With time we mean how much time it would take for an entrant to become a credible threat to the current competitors in the industry, and with money we mean the net present cost for reaching the same goal.

Industry growth

High growth in an industry always makes a company in a specific industry worth more. The industry growth can be said to consist of two variables: general GDP growth and industry-specific growth. High growth in an industry is attractive for two reasons. Firstly, it means that the market is expanding and that the company can keep or even lose some of its relative market share and still increase its revenues and potentially its profits. In industries with low or negative growth, companies have to fight for market share, often resulting in price wars and hence lower margins and profits. Secondly, industry growth indicates that the industry is in a dynamic phase, which can result in new industry segments and hence new opportunities for the company quickly to become the market leader and achieve a monopoly-like position. High industry growth often gives the companies in the industry opportunities to create positions where they can enjoy high returns.

Various market research firms or industry bodies measure industry growth on a continuous basis and estimates can be obtained from them.

Intellectual capital value drivers

There are four separate parts of intellectual capital, as illustrated by the value tree presented previously. These are human, customer, innovation and process capital. These areas cover all of the potential sources of intellectual capital in a company. Below we explain the most important value driver for each area.

Brand strength

Customer capital can be defined as the combined net present value of the company's customer relationships. Of course, this can be measured in many different ways. However, what is often considered most important is the loyalty of the current customer base and the company's ability to attract new customers. Customer loyalty is important because it is usually closely connected to profitability. It is generally significantly more expensive to acquire new customers than to increase revenues from existing ones. The ability to recruit new customers is important as it gives the potential growth rate in the customer base and market share. A good way of estimating these two variables and subsequently the customer capital is to analyze the strength of the brand.

> Customer loyalty is important because it is usually closely connected to profitability

Brands are important for a number of reasons. Firstly, globalization makes markets larger and more accessible. At the same time, the number of competitors is increasing and there are no protective customs duties or tariffs behind which to hide. In this fierce battle for customers, a strong brand is a very effective weapon since it can differentiate a producer's products or services from others and tilt the battle to the advantage of the brand owner.

Another reason why brands are becoming more and more important is 'technological convergence'. This means that a competitive advantage of a product, service or concept is seldom long-lived. Shortly after the launch of an innovative new product or service, competitors will have copied it and launched it under their own name. The result is that few products are truly unique. The only difference then is the brand, which becomes a decisive factor for the customer. This syndrome is enhanced by IT development and increased mobility of the workforce, which means that product development and copying of products is becoming faster all the time.

A third reason is that a brand can provide the owner with some competitive protection as it functions as a strong barrier to entry. In a market where the existing players have strong brands with a high degree of loyalty it will be very costly for a new player to enter the market. Try to imagine establishing yourself in the soft-drinks industry with a product competing with Coca-Cola and Pepsi Cola! Certainly, it is extremely expensive to buy mind space from your potential customers, something several soft-drink manufacturers have learned.

In addition, the brand, in contrast to human capital, is owned by the company and functions as the company's way of 'owning' the relationship with the customers. Brands tend to stand the test of time and often outlive the products that they launched in the beginning. IBM was, to take an example, a brand for industrial scales to start with. Furthermore, strong brands allow the company to extract a higher price, making an above-average return possible.

A way of measuring the strength of a brand is to combine two parameters: brand loyalty and brand recognition. Brand loyalty reflects the company's ability to keep existing customers and is measured, for instance, by the percentage of repeat customers. Brand recognition is an assessment of the company's potential to win new customers. We measure this, for example, by the percentage of the company's target group who recognize the company's brand and what it stands for.

Management and board competence and motivation

Human capital consists of the collective abilities, relationships, talents, knowledge and experience within the company. The principal difference between the company's human capital and structural capital is that human capital is not owned by the company.

The analysis of human capital can be divided up into both competence and motivation. In the analysis of human capital, special attention and focus should be given to the company's management and board.

Both the board and management deserve analysis, as they are interdependent. A below-par board can ruin good management of the company and poor management can hamper a greatly superior board. Similarly, motivation is of great importance as competence alone is not enough to guarantee good results. The reverse is also true; if the company board and management are completely incompetent then the level of motivation is really of little significance. Motivation can be divided into two parts: financial motivation, in the form of options, cash bonuses or other similar performance-related rewards, and the general working environment or atmosphere within the company.

A suggestion for measuring competence is through assessing the board and management's past performance according to some key financial value driver. The idea is that past performance often (but not always) tends to say a lot about future performance. In order to measure the motivation level we suggest the measurement of the percentage of compensation directly or indirectly linked to value creation combined with the personnel turnover at management level.

Innovation power

When analyzing a company's future prospects in the marketplace, the company's ability to renew itself and break new ground is of crucial importance. Innovation power is a measure of exactly this; a company's ability to improve its current products, develop completely new ones or develop a product that can take the company into a completely new industry segment.

The importance of innovation power has increased in past decades as a result of shortened product lifecycles

The importance of innovation power has increased in past decades as a result of shortened product lifecycles. A similar development can be observed in most growth industries where the ability of companies to create new products and services, i.e. their innovation power, is often decisive for their future success (e.g. the mobile phone industry).

A suggestion for measuring innovation power is to identify how high a percentage of the company's revenues originate from products and services launched over the past two, three years. In this manner you measure not only how good the company is at developing new products and services, but also how good the company is in getting these products to market and creating revenue streams based on their innovations.

Person-independent knowledge

Eleven days after McDonald's has signed a contract with a franchisee, the new restaurant is built and ready to serve hamburgers. The process of building a restaurant has become refined over the years and been documented down to the last detail. This is an example of how to create person-independent knowledge, an important part of a company's process capital.

Person-independent knowledge is valuable for two reasons. Firstly, the company owns this type of knowledge and the knowledge does not leave the company when employees do. Because of this, it is attributed lower risk than pure human capital. Secondly, the company can leverage person-independent knowledge better than it can leverage human capital. The reason for this is that person-independent knowledge can be used at the same time by many people and can be easily distributed. If McDonald's had only one building constructor with the aforementioned knowledge, they could build only one restaurant every 11th day. Through having this knowledge in the form of a digital manual it can be used in a large number of places simultaneously.

We suggest measuring person-independent knowledge through IT investment per employee multiplied by IT use per employee. It is not a perfect measure, but usually person-independent knowledge can be thought of as being closely related to the investments a company makes in IT. Of course, if this technology is not used then it is not worth anything. Therefore, a combination of investment and actual usage captures at least to some extent what we wish to have measured.

Framework for the underlying analysis

We have suggested how to structure the underlying analysis. The model consists of three parts: one external part, one internal part and a link between the two, the strategy. Then we presented seven key value drivers in the respective areas. The final model for the underlying analysis can be presented as shown in Figure 7.5.

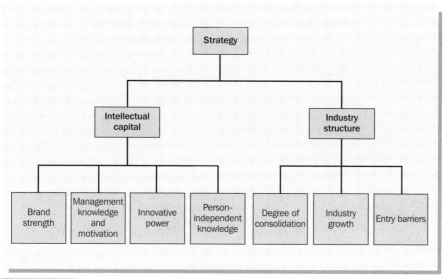

FIGURE 7.5   Model for the underlying analysis

This model is intended to give you inspiration and a way of thinking when trying to understand a business. It will also give you a good overview of the company's present and future status and will, it is hoped, make it easier to perform your underlying analysis. Furthermore, by structuring the underlying analysis, the valuation can be more correct and you will have a good foundation to stand on when you have to justify your valuation.

As we mentioned earlier, there could very well be key value drivers other than the seven presented here, and which are more applicable to the company you wish to value. It is up to you to choose the ones you believe best fits your industry and company.

Temporary monopolies – an additional tool for the underlying analysis

The framework that we developed in the preceding section is a suggestion for how to capture the underlying value drivers in a company, structure them in an appropriate way, and formalize them into a useful conceptual framework.

As mentioned, from a value perspective, a highly desirable characteristic of a company is either a completely unique product or service, and/or a dominant position in a certain industry. In other words, investors search for companies with some type of monopoly situation. As the man sometimes referred to as 'the world's greatest investor', Warren Buffett, explains in the book *Buffettology*[3] his primary criterion for deciding whether a company represents an investment opportunity is through deciding whether it enjoys what he calls consumer monopoly.

So, if this variable is of such interest to investors, how do you measure it? As of today, there are no commonly known and used models for evaluating monopolies. More specifically, there are no available frameworks for analysis regarding monopolies when conducting a valuation.

A reason for the lack of analytical models is perhaps that monopolies have not been a favourite subject among economists in recent decades. This is probably due to the stigma attached to the term 'monopoly', with government-regulated industries and decreased competition, which clearly result in disadvantages for consumers. The monopolies favoured by investors are not government regulated, however, but are driven instead by innovation and high growth. The early work of the Austrian economist Joseph Schumpeter postulated that monopoly should not be regarded as a failure in the competitive capital market but instead as a driver of economic development. He argued that it is the possibility of establishing a monopoly that encourages the entrepreneur to invent and capitalize their products or services. Monopolies in competitive environments, being without government regulations and other artificial barriers to entry, will not last for long and may therefore be regarded as temporary. The entrepreneur will then have to go on to the next industry or segment and try to create a new temporary monopoly.[4]

The basic idea is that a company's success is dependent largely on its ability to create and sustain temporary monopolies. When discussing the term 'monopoly', it is important to note that we refer to a monopoly when a company has a significant dominant position in a certain industry, sub-industry or segment. A monopoly in a highly consolidated industry might require 60–70 per cent market share, but only 20 per cent may be required in a highly fragmented industry where all other competitors have only one to two per cent market share. The traditional definition of monopoly[5]

---

[3] Buffett and Clark, 1997. (See Further reading.)

[4] For further reading about 'Schumpeter's hypothesis', as it is sometimes called, see *Market structure and innovation*, Kamien, M.I. and Schwartz, N.L., Cambridge, Cambridge University Press, 1984 and *Joseph A. Schumpeter: The economics and sociology of capitalism*, Swedberg, R., Princeton, Princeton University Press, 1991, pp. 157–8, or the original work: Schumpeter, *Theory of Economic Development*, 1936.

[5] For a definition of monopoly, see for example *Economics*, 6th edition, Parkin, M., Boston, Addison Wesley, 2002.

Note that we refer to a monopoly when a company has a significant dominant position in a certain industry

as an industry situation involving only one company is referred to as an absolute monopoly.

Below we present a framework for analyzing companies from a monopoly standpoint, which can be used to gain additional input when conducting a valuation.

Current temporary monopolies

The first question is how to measure the monopoly. At first, it may seem obvious that a company's market share provides a more or less exact indication of the degree of monopoly in any market. This only gives half the picture, however. Consider an example with two companies in different industries, both with a 30 per cent market share. Obviously, these two companies are big and important players in their respective industries. But how important are they? One of the companies has a competitor with 45 per cent of the market and the other has several small competitors with only one to two per cent market share each. Clearly, the latter company is in a stronger market position and can charge higher prices for its products/ services. In other words, the latter company has a stronger monopoly position than the former. This example explains why market share alone does not give enough information to measure the degree of monopoly.

Another candidate for the measurement of the degree of monopoly is the level of consolidation, i.e. number of competitors in the industry. Here, we face exactly the same problems as with market share. A consolidated industry of only three players might indicate a favourable position for the company analyzed, if it is the dominant one of those three companies. In that case, degree of consolidation gives a good indication of the monopoly situation. It is also possible, however, that one of the competitors has 70 per cent of the industry and the other two (including the company analyzed) split the remaining 30 per cent. In this case, the degree of consolidation presents a completely false picture of the monopoly situation for the company.

In order to reach a suitable measure, the market share and the level of consolidation need to be combined, resulting in what is generally called relative market share. We define relative market share as follows:

$$\text{Relative market share} = \frac{\text{company market share in per cent}}{\text{the sum of the market shares for the 4 largest competitors}}$$

Using relative market share captures the strength of a monopoly with 20 per cent market share if no one else in the industry has over one per cent. It also captures the strength of a monopoly with 80 per cent market share in a highly consolidated industry of only three companies. Note that, mathematically, a company approaches a monopoly when the relative market share approaches one. Thus, the closer the relative market share gets to one, the closer the company is to having an absolute monopoly.

Degree of temporary monopoly can be measured by the company's relative market share in the industry, sub-industry, or segment

Finding a way to measure a company's temporary monopoly is certainly a good start but only gives a static picture of the situation. One also needs to know the dynamics around the monopoly and how they will develop in the future. As the term 'temporary' suggests, monopolies in a competitive environment will not be sustained forever. The reason for this is that the profits made by the monopolist (as mentioned earlier, we assume the monopolist is efficient and thus utilizes their position to lower costs and increase prices) will attract other companies to the industry, thereby increasing the competition. What one needs to establish is the strength of the monopoly or, more specifically, the sustainability of the monopoly. The profits made by the monopolist will, as mentioned, attract new companies to the industry, if they can enter. What could potentially stop the inflow of companies to the industry is something that makes it harder for them to enter the industry, i.e. barriers to entry. Barriers to entry need to be examined closely since they determine the sustainability of the temporary monopoly.

The sustainability of the company's temporary monopoly can be measured by the level of barriers to entry to the industry, sub-industry or segment

The information given by the relative market share and barriers to entry thus gives an analytical framework for the analysis of the company's current temporary monopoly. Note that the analysis should be conducted for each of the company's businesses to give an indication of the company's total position. Also, it should be conducted with different industry definitions. Not even a company like Coca-Cola has a monopoly in the soft-drink industry. However, limiting the industry to the cola drink segment changes the picture and Coca-Cola could perhaps be said to have a sort of monopoly.

The analysis of the existence and the sustainability of a company's temporary monopoly can be visualized as shown in Figure 7.6. The figure shows the relative market share on the horizontal axis, where the higher the relative market share of the company (the closer the ratio is to one), the further to the right it is positioned. The vertical axis shows the total barriers to entry to the industry, where the greater the barriers to entry to the industry analyzed, the further up one moves on the vertical axis. The 45-degree line indicates that the further to the top right, the greater and the more sustainable is the company's temporary monopoly. In short, the further to the top right a company lies, the more attractive the business from a monopoly standpoint.

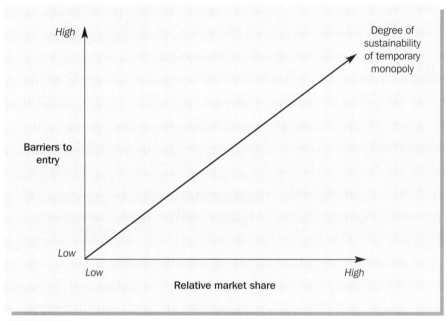

FIGURE 7.6   Current temporary monopolies

So, what does a temporary monopoly really tell us about a company's operations? Well, consider a company plotted in the lower-right corner of the diagram. That company has a high relative market share and thus a temporary monopoly. In value creation terms, it is quite probable that the company is delivering high cash flows to its shareholders. This implies that the company should be highly valued. However, as could be observed from the DCF framework it is the future cash flows that are to be valued.

In the example, the company is in an industry with low barriers to entry indicating that it is easy for new companies to enter the arena. In other words, the company's temporary monopoly is not that sustainable and the risk is high that neither are the cash flows it currently generates for its shareholders. If the company had the same relative market share but enjoyed higher industry barriers to entry (in the figure, if the company were higher on the vertical axis), the company would, all other things being equal, have more stable cash flows and thus a higher value. From an investor's perspective, the current candidate might be an interesting company to buy, if one could increase the barriers to entry or if one believes someone else will increase them. Means for increasing barriers to entry include achieving economies of scale, building brand loyalty or binding the important suppliers and distributors closer to you.

> The greater and more sustainable the temporary monopoly, the higher and more stable the cash flows and thus the higher the value of the company's operations

Consider now a company in the upper-left corner of the diagram. Such a company is in an industry with high barriers to entry and thus the industry is likely to be protected from new entrants. The company does not, however, have a dominant position in the industry. There are other companies in the industry with significantly higher relative market share. The company can thus not be said to have a monopoly. A company with a higher relative market share (in the figure, further to the right), would, all other things being equal, have larger cash flows and thus a higher value. From an investor perspective, this might be an interesting company to buy if one believes that the company will or can increase its relative market share.

Future temporary monopolies

The degree and sustainability of a temporary monopoly can give some guide to the value of the company's current operations. This does not, however, involve any analysis of future cash flows coming from outside the current operations. The above example only illustrates existing temporary monopolies and their sustainability, but gives no information about the company's opportunities for new temporary monopolies. Again, the term 'temporary' implies that the monopoly will not last forever and therefore it is important for valuation purposes to examine further the company's ability to create new temporary monopolies. Thus, an additional tool is needed for analyzing potential future temporary monopolies.

The company's ability to establish temporary monopolies in the future is, of course, to a large extent dependent upon the company itself. It is dependent on the company's ability to develop the new products and services that will somehow give birth to a new sub-industry or segment, and furthermore, the ability to commercialize products/services and to

The company's resources for creating future temporary monopolies can be approximated by its innovative power, measured as sales from new products/services (over the last three years) in relation to total sales

achieve a dominant position in that industry. This ability is what we earlier in this chapter referred to as 'innovative power'. Product lifecycles have become shorter and shorter in today's competitive environment, meaning that the company's innovative power becomes even more important. As mentioned in the earlier discussion, we suggest measuring the innovative power by looking at sales from new products/services (over the past three years) in relation to total sales.

Suppose now that a company has all the innovative power necessary to create unique products and services. Will it then automatically be able to create future temporary monopolies? Unfortunately, it is not that simple and we must also consider the company's environment.

Industrial dynamics provides opportunities for creating future temporary monopolies and can be approximated and measured by industry growth

Simply put, there must be industrial opportunities for the establishment of temporary monopolies as well as internal possibilities. In order for a company to create a new temporary monopoly, a new sub-industry or segment needs to be established. The degree to which new segments and sub-industries are created can be called the degree of dynamics in the industry. We can approximate the dynamics of the industry using industry growth.

High-growth industries tend to give rise to more industry opportunities than low-growth industries. Since the creation of new temporary monopolies depends largely on new segments or sub-industries being created, the higher the growth, the greater the industrial opportunities for future temporary monopolies.

Figure 7.7 shows how well-equipped the company is internally for creating future temporary monopolies, as well as the industry opportunities for future creation of temporary monopolies. The horizontal axis shows the industrial opportunities through industry growth. The higher the industry growth and the greater the industrial opportunities for temporary monopoly, the further to the right is the industry in the figure. The vertical axis shows the company's innovative power through measuring the company's sales from new products/services in relation to total sales. The higher up on the vertical axis, the higher the innovative power and the greater the internal capacity for the creation of temporary monopolies. The 45-degree line indicates the combined (internal and industrial) opportunities for future temporary monopolies; the further to the top right it lies, the greater the opportunities.

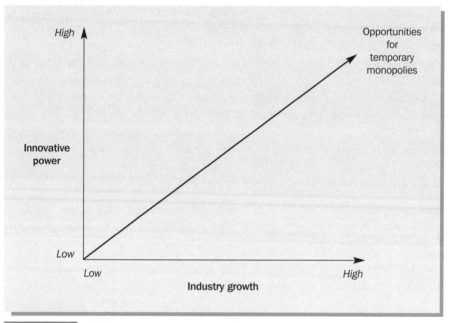

FIGURE 7.7   Future temporary monopolies

What does the diagram tell us about future opportunities for the company? Consider a company in the lower-right corner of the figure. The company is in a high-growth industry with many opportunities for the creation of new temporary monopolies. The company, however, has low or no innovation power. It cannot produce new products or services that take advantage of the industrial opportunities. Clearly, another company in the same industry but with higher innovative power (and thus a higher position on the vertical axis) would have better opportunities for future temporary monopolies. Because of that, and assuming similar operations, the latter company's probability of future cash flows from new temporary monopolies is higher. Thus, all things being equal, the value of that company will be higher.

> The greater the possibilities for future temporary monopolies, the greater the probability of unexpected increases in the company's cash flow and therefore the higher the value of the company's future opportunities

Consider next a company in the upper-left corner. That company almost drowns in its innovative power, but since there is low industry growth, there are few industrial opportunities for new temporary monopolies. The company is innovative in the wrong industry. Another company with the same innovative power, but in another industry with higher growth and thus more industrial opportunities, will clearly have larger opportunities for future temporary monopolies. That company will possess a higher probability of being able to establish future temporary monopolies and therefore will have a higher probability of receiving increases in its future cash flow. That company will therefore also have a higher value.

Summary

In this chapter, we have discussed the importance of the underlying analysis and of understanding the value creation within the company by identifying so-called value drivers. The analysis of the key value drivers is crucial for correctly determining the input variables in a DCF analysis.

One can distinguish between financial value drivers such as operating margins or return on invested capital and operational, non-financial value drivers. Generally, financial value drivers are fairly generic while operational value drivers vary from company to company and from industry to industry.

Consequently, we presented a framework for the underlying analysis of key value drivers, where we divided the analysis into three distinct areas – the company's internal resources, its intellectual capital; the company's external environment, its industry structure; and the company's strategy. Seven key value drivers, which have been shown to often have significant impact on corporate value, were described within the fields of intellectual capital and industry structure. Company strategy does not include any value drivers, but can be seen as the way the company chooses to exploit its key value drivers within intellectual capital and industry structure.

The four key value drivers in intellectual capital are brand strength, innovation power, management and board motivation and past performance, and person-independent knowledge. In the industry structure, the key value drivers are sector growth, relative market share (the market share of the company in relation to its competitors) and barriers to entry.

Finally, we introduced the concept of temporary monopoly as a different analytical tool for analyzing a company's underlying business. We distinguished between current temporary monopoly and future temporary monopoly. A current temporary monopoly is measured by the company's relative market share and barriers to entry, thereby estimating the current market position and its sustainability. Future temporary monopoly is measured by innovative power and sector growth and gives an indication of the potential for new temporary monopolies.

In the next chapter, we are going to put our hard-won skills to practical use when we use the concepts and techniques we have discussed to value a company in practice.

8

How to value your company in practice – an example

What topics are covered in this chapter?

- Underlying analysis of Mobitronics
- DCF valuation of Mobitronics
- Scenario analysis
- Checking the underlying assumptions
- Multiple-based valuation of Mobitronics
- Piecing it all together – the value of the company
- Summary

After reading this far you will hopefully have a fundamental theoretical understanding of how to value a company. Now it is time to put everything into practice by valuing our example company, Mobitronics, presented earlier.

Most investors, analysts and other professionals have their own preferred way of conducting a valuation. When you are choosing how to do yours, there are three major considerations to be taken into account:

1. **Purpose of valuation.** As shown in Chapter 3, there are a number of different situations or scenarios where you need a valuation of a company – for example, acquisitions, investment opportunities or stock-based incentive programmes. In each situation, you have to decide on how detailed and exact the valuation needs to be.

> When doing valuations, it is important to consider the purpose of the valuation, available time and resources as well as available data. Usually, there is a trade-off between effort and accuracy

2 Available time and energy. What resources are available for the exercise? For all different types of valuation, the more thoroughly you perform the underlying analysis and the more carefully you estimate assumptions, the more accurate the valuation is likely to be. But, as always, there is a trade-off between resources, complexity and accuracy.

3 Data input availability. How much data can you get hold of? If you, for example, wish to do a full DCF valuation, you will need reliable and updated current and forecasted financial information. If no or little financial data are available, it might be better to use a valuation approach, such as multiples, requiring fewer data.

In order for you to make your choice easier, we give three examples of different levels of valuations.

1 The easiest and fastest valuation approach is a pure relative one where the company's value is compared and calculated using multiples from other traded comparable companies.

2 The second approach is a combination of fundamental multiples and relative multiples where you check the company's valuation relative to its peers as well as its fundamentals.

3 Finally, in cases when you wish to really understand the company and its valuation, we recommend doing a standalone valuation, such as a DCF valuation with an underlying analysis of the company's business and its environment focusing on its key value drivers. The DCF input variables should also be checked for reasonableness and a relative and fundamental multiple valuation should be performed to complement the DCF valuation.

When performing a valuation, there is often a trade-off between time spent and achieved level of accuracy and certainty (see Figure 8.1).

In this chapter we will carry out a valuation as described under item 3 above. To begin with, we need to forecast income statements and balance sheets for the explicit period. This part is crucial to the outcome of the valuation as it determines many important input data.

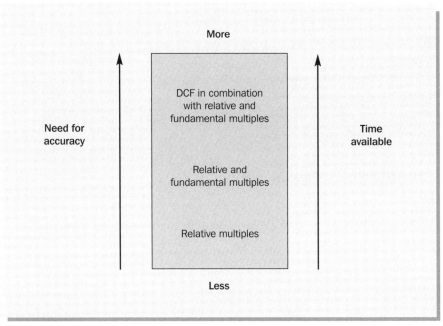

More

DCF in combination
with relative and
fundamental multiples

Need for
accuracy

Time
available

Relative and
fundamental multiples

Relative multiples

Less

FIGURE 8.1   Deciding which model(s) to use

Forecasting is the art of using history and the present to predict the future. Research has shown that short-term predictions can be quite accurate but that they become less accurate the further into the future you are trying to forecast. Therefore, a good rule of thumb for your forecasts should be that no bold assumptions are made for the long run.

> A good rule of thumb for your forecasts should be that no bold assumptions are made for the long run

A common approach when forecasting financials is to start with historical data to analyze key ratios such as revenue growth, margins, working capital levels, etc. A base case would be to assume that the historical trends continue for the years of the explicit period and then make adjustments based on your analysis of the company/industry/economy. In addition to this, it is often wise to analyze competitors' historical financial records with regards to the same key ratios to look for deviances that may present opportunities for improvement or risks of deterioration.

In many cases, the above is the only basis for forecasting. In some cases you may wish to use a more comprehensive approach. For a fundamental understanding of Mobitronics as a company and the industry in which it operates, we will perform an underlying analysis using the model presented in the previous chapter. This analysis, used in conjunction with Mobitronics and its competitors' historical figures, provides the basis when forecasting the income statements, balance sheets and the other assumptions for the DCF model.

Underlying analysis of Mobitronics

There are many ways to go about the underlying analysis and many potential variables to analyze. However, as mentioned previously in Chapter 7, seven key value variables have been shown to be of specific importance in many companies and industries. It is important to view these variables as a guideline to start from and not as an exact model. It may be perfectly in order to exclude some of the seven variables from the analysis and some others may need to be added. Obviously, it depends on the specific industry and company you want to analyze.

Brand

The analysis of the company's brand can be divided into two parts: brand loyalty and brand awareness. In practice, one can measure the brand's strength in a number of ways but we suggest:

> **Brand loyalty**: percentage repeat customers

and

> **Brand awareness**: percentage in the company's target group who recognize the company's brand

Companies usually have access to information on brand awareness and the number of repeat customers. For Mobitronics, research showed that 65 per cent of the company's target group recognized the company's brand and that 85 per cent of Mobitronics' customers were repeat buyers.

These numbers leave the impression of a well-positioned company with a good relationship to its existing customers. The average churn rate in the industry is around 20 per cent, which means that Mobitronics is slightly better at keeping its customers than its competitors. This shows that Mobitronics' differentiation strategy works well and that the customers are happy with the product quality and level of service.

Quite often, customer churn or customer loyalty data are important for an analysis of the company's cost for future growth since it is generally much more expensive to attract a new customer than to keep an old one. As Mobitronics acquires new customers, it is likely that they will become repeat (and, therefore, profitable) customers. In addition, since the number of repeat customers is high, the expected lifetime revenue per customer is high, thereby increasing the value of launching new products or services.

Management and board past performance and motivation

Given the soft nature of this variable, it can be very hard to estimate. As mentioned in the previous chapter on this, we believe that a combination of track record and motivation captures most of the important features of this variable. Hence, a suggestion on how to measure management past performance and motivation is:

Management and board past performance: choose any financial indicator for the current or a previous company that you find appropriate given the nature of the business and see how it developed under current management and board

Management and board motivation: percentage of performance-based remuneration and staff turnover at management level

In the case of Mobitronics, the management and board have demonstrated significant expertise and skill in building and managing the company over the last seven years. They have successfully chosen a strategic direction and achieved a fine return on investment. As such, given that past performance is as good an indicator as we can get of future performance, the management and board are important assets going forward.

As regards motivation, all key individuals in the management and board have considerable shareholdings and are part of a long-term option scheme in the company. Thus, a large portion of the management team's personal assets is tied up in Mobitronics' securities. Fixed compensation is also relatively low and represents about 40 per cent of total compensation. Instead, management and board have cash bonuses based on a combination of company cash flows and turnover. In other words, there is no doubt that the management team has large over time financial incentives for the company to succeed. If things go badly, the management team will receive relatively low salaries and they risk losing all the money they have invested in the company. From a valuation perspective, this is positive, partly because it ties the management to the company and partly because it aligns the incentives for the management and board with those of the shareholders. Finally, staff turnover has been low in management as well as in the rest of the company. This indicates a good working environment and personnel policy, thereby further decreasing the risk of important people leaving the organization.

Innovation power

The power to innovate new products or services is often an important characteristic, especially for companies in high-growth and/or innovative sectors. This is because existing products quickly become obsolete and new products need to replace them. Innovation power does not usually affect sales or cash flow in the short term, but it is one of the most important variables when determining long-term competitiveness of the company. The previous chapter provided a suggestion for measuring innovation power:

$$\text{Innovation power} = \frac{\text{proportion of sales from new products}}{\text{total sales}}$$

The definition of new products obviously varies from industry to industry depending on how often new products come on to the market in the industry. In the mobile provider sector, for example, the product cycle seldom lasts more than a few years, while for pharmaceuticals it can be decades.

Mobitronics' innovation power appears to be strong. Two new product areas have been launched in the past two years – mobile broadband and mobile data services. Both of these have generated significant revenues from customers, and the mobile broadband especially has been a financial success. A closer examination reveals that the proportion of new product sales (released during the previous two years)/total sales accounted for almost 20 per cent of Mobitronics' total sales last year.

Person-independent knowledge

As mentioned in the previous chapter, person-independent knowledge is difficult to quantify and measure and varies a lot from industry to industry. Earlier, we said that the proposed means of measuring person-independent knowledge was:

Person-independent knowledge: IT investment in relation to turnover and usage of IT investment by customers, employees and suppliers in their dealings with the company

Mobitronics has worked hard to reduce its dependence on people and to automate and computerize company processes wherever possible. To begin with, the favourable customer relationships, which are behind the high level of repeat purchases, are dealt with by a computerized customer-support system. The customer database and all customer contact are based on a CRM platform, which has somewhat shifted the customer relationship from the employees to the company. Mobitronics' investment in IT in relation to revenues has been about 5 per cent over the past three years. This is slightly higher than its competitors, and fits with the image Mobitronics has as a technologically advanced company. In addition, the purchasing function is internet-based and orders are sent automatically when stocks reach a certain level, while sales are mostly generated through the company's own stores and through resellers. The individuals working in these stores all represent a small part of the company's sales so the loss of one salesperson does not in any way threaten the overall sales for the company. Mobitronics seems relatively independent of specific individuals and this reduces operational risk.

The knowledge in the management and board is, however, harder to transform into a digital form and make person-independent, which makes Mobitronics dependent on them staying with the company. The company is aware of this, however, and since the entire management team are shareholders with strong incentives to stay, this threat is not viewed as especially great.

Sector growth

Industry or sector growth is frequently defined as the total growth in sales for a given industry. This is often measured by industry organizations, market research companies, investment bank analysts or by the companies themselves.

Generally, industry growth comes from two sources – an increasing number of customers or increased revenue per customer. In the mobile sector over the course of a number of years, growth came mainly from new customers entering the mobile market. In the future, however, growth will increasingly have to come from increased revenues per customer, simply because most people in Mobitronic's markets already have a mobile phone. The 15–20 per cent growth that has characterized the industry historically is unlikely to be seen in the future and analysts expect the market to grow by 10–11 per cent until 2013. Mobitronics has historically been able to defend its market share and is expected to do so in the future as well. After that period, however, the forecasts become more difficult as the introduction of the next generation of mobile networks will have significant impact on the industry landscape. Though the future seems shrouded in mist, the general assumptions from analysts regarding revenues are that Mobitronics will keep its market share and that lifetime revenue per user will increase as consumers utilize the enlarged portfolio of mobile services provided. The downside is that as competition increases, customer acquisition costs will go up and margins will be reduced. Analysts in general believe the long-term growth in the industry to be 4–5 per cent.

Level of consolidation

The level of consolidation is generally a good indication of how competitive a given industry is. A proposed method of measuring both how competitive a given industry is, as well as how strong a company's position is in the industry, is to measure the relative market share for the company in question:

> **Relative market share**: the company's market share in sales in relation to the four largest competitors' market share combined

Analysis of the level of consolidation will give a hint as to the level of margins the company has maintained and will be allowed to maintain in the future. Certainly, the level of consolidation depends on how one chooses to define the industry under analysis. For Mobitronics our definition of the market is: 'all companies that sell mobile network capacity or mobile services to end-users'. In most countries, the mobile sector is an oligopoly dominated by a few companies, with the former state-owned Telco as the market leader. This is expected to change as the mobile operator industry becomes more international and with the introduction of the fourth-generation (4G) mobile networks, increasing competition in the industry and decreasing margins.

The current competitive situation is, however, beneficial for Mobitronics and margins are high. Mobitronics has about 22 per cent market share and an identical 22 per cent in relative market share since four companies have

100 per cent of the market. The EBITDA margin is about 44 per cent and is expected to be sustainable as long as the industry structure remains intact. As 4G is introduced this is expected to change. Long-term EBITDA margins are then assumed to drop to approximately 30 per cent.

Barriers to entry

The level of consolidation indicates the current competitiveness in the industry but does not give any information about how stable the current industry structure is. Therefore, we need to analyze the industry's barriers to entry, which gives a great deal of information about potential future industry evolution and how stable the current competitive situation is in an industry. The most common way to measure barriers to entry is:

Barriers to entry: time and cost required to establish a competing firm in the industry

Current barriers to entry are large, to say the least, for a new entrant. One would need to invest heavily in mobile networks, sales, customer support, product development, etc. It would take a long time and the costs would be significant. However, as there is a complete technological shift coming up, an opportunity for competition might arise. In order to be able to provide 4G services, a third-generation (3G) firm like Mobitronics must build a completely new network. This means that the old infrastructure network investments are no longer a barrier to entry for a competitor. However, the investment in becoming a full-service 3G provider in a small market is expected to cost between €800m and €1,000m and take about three years. Therefore, there is little probability of the advent of a fragmented market with lots of small competitors waging price wars and destroying profitability in the industry. Consequently, the current industry structure is well-protected until the first companies start offering 4G services predicted for launch during early 2011, and chances thereafter of a fairly concentrated market are also high.

DCF valuation of Mobitronics

Now with a deepened understanding of Mobitronics' business through the seven key value drivers, it is time to move on to the financial valuation in order to determine the theoretical value of Mobitronics. We use the so-called McKinsey version of a DCF valuation, as presented in Chapter 6, and go through the following five main steps to estimate the:

1 Weighted cost of capital – WACC.

2 Free cash flow for the explicit period.

3 Free cash flow for the hypergrowth period.

4 Terminal value.

5 Total value of Mobitronics.

Before we move into the first step we need historical (2009) as well as fore-casted (2010–2013) income statements and balance sheets, as provided in Table 8.1 opposite.

Step 1 Estimating cost of capital – WACC

The cost of capital corresponds to the risks inherent in the company's future cash flows. One can divide the risk in future cash flows into finan-cial risk (increased debt/equity ratio, decreased interest coverage, etc.) and operational risk (increased competition, decreased barriers to entry, etc.). Usually, it is desirable to balance risks against each other so that a com-pany with high operational risks has lower financial risks and vice versa.

WACC (weighted average cost of capital) is the average cost of capital for the equity and debt. It is calculated using the following formula:

$$WACC = \frac{E}{D+E} \times C_E + \frac{D}{D+E} \times C_D \times (1-T)$$

where E is the market value of equity, D is the market value of debt, C_E is the cost of equity, C_D is the cost of debt and T is the tax rate.

Optimal capital structure

The first step in determining the WACC is to assess the company's long-term optimal capital structure (which usually is not likely to be the current one if the industry is not very mature). Since Mobitronics has a relatively simple capital structure involving only common equity and simple debt type financing, we only need to analyze the debt/equity ratio (in case of more complicated financing structures with mezzanine debt or convertible debentures the principles are the same but the procedure varies; for details on this we refer to the literature in the Further reading section at the end of this book).

Table 8.1: Mobitronics' historic (2009) and forecasted (2010–2013) income statement and balance sheet

Income statement (€m) Year	2009	2010	2011	2012	2013
Revenues	4,640	5,313	5,897	6,388	6,993
Growth (%)	11	15	11	8	9
Operating costs	−2,586	−3,025	−3,391	−3,868	−4,201
Growth (%)	10	17	12	14	9
EBITDA	2,054	2,288	2,506	2,520	2,792
Depreciation	−434	−542	−675	−778	−881
EBIT	1,620	1,746	1,831	1,742	1,911
Interest expenses	−31	−35	−52	−157	−188
Interest income	21	23	40	73	94
Net income (pre-tax)	1,610	1,734	1,819	1,658	1,817
Taxes	−453	−498	−529	−507	−546
Net income (post-tax)	1,157	1,236	1,290	1,151	1,271
Balance sheet (€m) Year	2009	2010	2011	2012	2013
Goodwill	73	58	43	27	11
Net property, plant and equipment	2,771	3,224	4,364	8,102	8,567
Accounts receivable and other current assets	971	937	1,135	1,229	1,746
Cash in bank	36	818	1,591	1,881	1,834
Total assets	3,851	5,037	7,133	11,239	12,158
Stockholders' equity	2,045	2,873	4,112	5,210	5,908
Deferred income taxes	482	416	845	1,539	1,248
Interest-bearing liabilities	245	516	808	2,008	2,508
Accounts payable and other liabilities	1,079	1,232	1,368	2,482	2,494
Total liabilities and equity	3,851	5,037	7,133	11,239	12,158

$$\text{Debt to equity ratio} = \frac{\text{debt}}{\text{shareholders' equity}}$$

The process of assessing the long-term capital structure has four parts, analyzing the following:

1   The current capital structure based on market values.
2   Capital structures of comparable companies.
3   The likely future capital structure based on the company's financing policies and corporate strategy.
4   The capital structure that achieves the lowest possible WACC while providing enough interest coverage and a beneficial balance between operative and financial risk.

Firstly, we calculate the current debt/equity ratio based on market values. As mentioned in Chapter 6, the debt needs to be adjusted (basically by adding or deducting the net present value of the difference between actual interest and the interest required to borrow the same amount today).

Market value of debt = debt on balance sheet

× reasonable adjustment to market value of debt

For Mobitronics, we estimate the market value of the debt to be the same as the book value of debt as the loans were refinanced very recently. A recently refinanced loan can be seen as a recently acquired asset; a market value has been established. Consequently, the market value of debt equals €245m.

The market value of equity is, in fact, what we are looking for by doing the DCF valuation. To solve the Descartian problem of circularity, we will use the value of the company's equity given by the stock market. The accumulated value of all company shares is generally called a company's market capitalization.

Market capitalization = price per share × number of shares outstanding

Here 40 × 409,692,300 = €16,387.7m

Based on the two numbers above, we simply divide interest-bearing debt by the market value of Mobitronics' equity.

$$\text{current debt to equity ratio of Mobitronics} = \frac{245}{16{,}387.7} = 0.01495 = 1.5\%$$

Secondly, we review the capital structures of the main competitors of Mobitronics. The average debt/equity ratio for these is 0.51, implying that Mobitronics has a significantly less aggressive capital structure than its competitors. In fact, the current capital structure of Mobitronics is extremely conservative.

Another data point worth analyzing is the development of the debt/equity ratio based on balance sheet values. Management has declared that it wishes to implement a more aggressive capital structure in the future. Looking at forecasted balance sheet values we can see that the projected debt/equity ratio at the end of the explicit forecast period in the year 2013 is 42.5 per cent (2,508/5,908), based on balance sheet values. This is almost four times more debt in relation to equity than in year 2009 with a debt/equity ratio based on balance sheet values of 11.98 per cent (245/2,045).

Assuming a debt/equity ratio of 0.42 would result in the following forecasted interest coverage:

$$\frac{\text{forecasted interest}}{\text{coverage}} = \frac{\text{forecasted EBITDA 2013}}{\text{forecasted interest expenses 2013}} = \frac{2{,}792}{188} = 14.85$$

Interest coverage of 14.85 is extremely safe, but appears reasonable considering the high operational risk and the potential large investments in new mobile systems or new market entries.

Finally, we estimate the highest possible debt/equity ratio subject to sufficient interest coverage. We will here define 'sufficient interest coverage' as 'investment grade', which means that the EBITDA needs to be minimally twice the size of the interest payments. This gives us the following equation:

$$\frac{2{,}792}{2} = 0.065 \times \text{debt, thus debt} = 21{,}477$$

Maximum debt/equity ratio with sufficient interest coverage based on balance sheet values is therefore:

$$\frac{\text{debt}}{\text{equity}} = \frac{21{,}477}{2{,}045} = 10.5$$

The debt can thus maximally exceed the equity by 10.5 times within the limits of the 'investment grade' definition. This, however, is an extreme case and would represent a too great financial risk exposure given the inherent risk in the operations.

So, given the four different levels of debt/equity ratios, we will use a target debt/equity ratio of 0.42 since:

- It gives the company the financing it needs – not more, not less.
- It is in line with management's operational risk assessment.
- It provides for sufficient interest coverage.
- It appears reasonable compared to the industry's debt/equity ratio.

Cost of capital – equity financing

The cost of equity financing is composed of two components – the risk-free interest and an additional yield that is appropriate for the level of risk of the equity. When determining the cost of equity, the so-called capital asset pricing model (CAPM) is commonly used:

Cost of equity = risk-free rate of return + (market risk premium × beta)

We will use the following numbers as input in our CAPM calculation:

- **The risk-free rate of return** – for Mobitronics we use a 10-year bond that yields 4 per cent.
- **The market risk premium** – as all of Mobitronics' operations and revenues are Europe-based and the stock is traded in Europe, we will use the European market risk premium in the fall of 2009, which was approximately 4.5 per cent.
- **The beta** – the publicly traded Mobitronics' share has a beta of 1.73.

Applying these numbers to the Mobitronics' equity gives us the following equation:

$$\text{cost of equity according to CAPM}$$
$$= 4\% + (4.5\% \times 1.73) = 0.188 = 11.8\%$$

Cost of debt

The cost of debt is the interest the company would have to pay if it had to attract more money from lenders. Hence, it is the current market cost of debt that should be used and not the historical cost at which the company has borrowed its money. In general, the cost of debt for companies with simple debt financing can be calculated as:

Cost of debt = risk-free rate of return + company risk premium

However, the best estimation of the current market cost of debt is, of course, if the company has recently borrowed money. In the case of Mobitronics, a majority of the current balance sheet debt was refinanced not long ago at the rate of 6.5 per cent, which is the cost of debt we will use in our calculations.

Calculating the WACC

When we have the target capital structure, the cost of equity and the cost of debt, we now apply the WACC formula to determine the cost of capital for Mobitronics. First, however, we need to translate the D/E ratio to the D/(E + D) ratio and the E/(E + D) ratio according to the following:

Taking the already computed D/E ratio of 0.42, we can calculate the E/D ratio as:

$$\frac{E}{D} = \frac{1}{D/E} = \frac{1}{0.42} = 2.38$$

Now that we have the absolutes for D and E (1 and 2.38) we can apply the WACC formula:

$$WACC = \frac{E}{D + E} \times C_E + \frac{D}{D + E} \times C_D \times (1 - T)$$

$$= \frac{2.38}{1 + 2.38} \times 0.118 + \frac{1}{1 + 2.38} \times 0.065 \times (1 - 0.3)$$

$$= 0.083 + 0.0135 = 0.0965 = 9.65\%$$

Based on the target long-term capital structure, the cost of equity and the cost of debt we estimate the weighted average cost of capital (WACC) for Mobitronics to be 9.65 per cent.

Step 2 Estimating free cash flow for the explicit period

Decide how long the explicit value period should be

Mobitronics is currently undergoing significant expansion and consequently growth in EBIT, changes in working capital and other key variables are expected to vary over the next four years. Therefore, we estimate that it is reasonable to calculate the free cash flow explicitly from 2010 to 2013. From 2014 to 2018, we forecast that Mobitronics will have a constant growth exceeding the long-term perpetuity growth, so-called hypergrowth.

Beginning year 2019 it is reasonable to believe that the company as well as the industry will be more mature and that growth in free cash flows will reach its long-term constant rate (i.e. its steady state). Note that in our example, fluctuations in working capital or investments are balanced by similar fluctuations in EBIT, which does not have to be the case in industries where companies due to economies of scale or entry barriers may enjoy a higher long-term ROIC through growing EBIT faster than working capital and investments.

Analyze and determine EBIT for years 2010–2013

The EBIT for 2010–2013 is obtained from the forecasted income statements. If no such forecast exists from the company, you will have to do the forecasts yourself based on whatever information you have at hand. As mentioned earlier, revenues are generally the most difficult to forecast. In the mobile industry, new customers signing up, as well as increasing revenue per customer, drive the growth in revenues and therefore EBIT. Mobitronics' positioning and existing barriers to entry lead us to expect the company to grow at least in line with the market. We therefore accept the company's revenue forecasts of 15 per cent growth in 2010, 11 per cent in 2011, 8 per cent in 2012 and 9 per cent in 2013. We also expect costs to grow in line with the company's estimates up to 2013.

The forecasted profit and loss account for Mobitronics for the years 2010–2013 is shown in Table 8.2.

Table 8.2: Forecasted profit and loss account for Mobitronics for the years 2010–2013 (amounts in €m)

Year	2010	2011	2012	2013
+Revenues	5,313	5,897	6,388	6,993
Growth (%)	15	11	8	9
–Costs	–3,025	–3,391	–3,868	–4,201
Growth (%)	17	12	14	9
EBITDA	2,288	2,506	2,520	2,792
Depreciation	–542	–675	–778	–881
EBIT	1,746	1,831	1,742	1,911

Estimate cash taxes on EBIT

As mentioned in Chapter 6, taxes from the income statement need to be transformed into taxes on EBIT. In a DCF model, the tax shield on interest expenses is instead accounted for in the calculation of the WACC (decreasing WACC and therefore increasing corporate value) and therefore the tax shield on interest expenses should be added back in the calculation of free cash flow. Mobitronics' taxes on EBIT for 2010–2013 are calculated as shown in Table 8.3.

Table 8.3 Mobitronics' taxes on EBIT for 2010–2013 (amounts in €m)

Year	2010	2011	2012	2013
Taxes from income statement	498	529	507	546
+ Tax shield on interest expense	10.5	15.6	47.1	56.4
– Tax on interest income	–6.9	–12	–21.9	–28.2
– Tax on non-operating income	0			
Cash taxes on EBIT	501.6	532.6	532.2	574.2

The computation of the tax shield on interest expense and income is quite straightforward. For example, in 2010 it is calculated as follows:

$$\text{tax rate} \times \text{interest payments} = 0.3 \times 35 = 10.5$$

And the tax on interest income is:

$$\text{tax rate} \times \text{interest income} = 0.3 \times 23 = 6.9$$

Depreciation expenses

Depreciation expenses include all costs deducted from EBIT, not representing a cash outflow from the company. Since depreciation expenses do not result in a capital outflow for the company but function only as an accounting procedure to spread investments over the lifetime of the asset, it should be added back to EBIT.

For Mobitronics we just take them directly from the income statement shown in Table 8.4.

Table 8.4: Mobitronics' income statement for 2010–2013 (amounts in €m)

Year	2010	2011	2012	2013
Depreciation	542	675	778	881

Estimate capital expenditure 2010–2013

When forecasting the income statement and balance sheet you will need to have a view on capital expenditure. Once you have forecasted the balance sheet, each year's capital expenditure can be calculated from the income statement and the balance sheet as the increase in net property, plant, equipment, machinery, etc. plus depreciation expense for the period. The increase in fixed assets is usually the most difficult item to forecast. An able way of thinking here is to assume that a certain amount of fixed assets is needed for each dollar of sales if no apparent economies of scale exist and no extraordinary investments are forecasted.

In the mobile industry, the major expected capital expenditure is the investment needed in the fourth-generation mobile networks. This investment is rather complex and we will simplify it somewhat. This means that investments from 2010 to 2013 are extraordinarily high and will from 2014 fall to lower investment levels in relation to revenues (see Table 8.5).

Table 8.5: Forecasted capital expenditure 2010–2013 (amounts in €m)

Year	2010	2011	2012	2013
+ Increase in net property, plant, equipment, etc.	453	1,140	3,738	465
+ Depreciation expense	542	675	778	881
Capital expenditure	**995**	**1,815**	**4,516**	**1,346**

Forecasted working capital for 2010–2013

Table 8.6 shows an assessment of the changes in Mobitronics' working capital for the years 2010–2013. Here, forecasting revenues is crucial, as fluctuations in working capital tend to correlate with changes in revenues.

Table 8.6: Forecasted change in working capital 2010–2013 (€m)

Year	2010	2011	2012	2013
+ Δ Cash in bank	782	773	290	–47
+ Δ Accounts receivable and other current assets	–34	198	94	517
– Δ Accounts payable and other non-interest-bearing liabilities	153	136	1,114	12
Changes in working capital	**595**	**835**	**–730**	**458**

Δ = increase/decrease

Investment in goodwill

The investment in goodwill represents the cost of acquiring assets or other companies in excess of their book value. The investment in goodwill is best calculated as the change in goodwill in the balance sheet between two years plus the amortization of goodwill in that year.

Mobitronics does not expect to carry out any acquisitions in the next few years and therefore no investment in goodwill is forecasted.

Estimate free cash flow for the explicit period 2010–2013 and discount it back to today

Forecasted cash flows for 2010–2013 can now be calculated and discounted back to today using the cost of capital derived earlier. Note that cash flow for the first year is discounted back one year, cash flow for year two is discounted back two years, etc. Then the discounted cash flows are added together. Do not forget to deduct potential losses in one year from potential profits in other years, as this will affect tax and therefore the free cash flow for each year (see Table 8.7).

Table 8.7: Present value of free cash flow 2010–2013 (€m)

Year	2010	2011	2012	2013
EBITDA	2,288	2,506	2,520	2,792
Depreciation	–542	–675	–778	–881
EBIT	1,746	1,831	1,742	1,911
Cash taxes on EBIT	–501.6	–532.6	–532.2	–574.2
NOPLAT	1,244.4	1,298.4	1,209.8	1,336.8
Depreciation	542	675	778	881
Gross cash flow	1,786.4	1,973.4	1,987.8	2,217.8
Capital expenditure	–995	–1,815	–4,516	–1,346
Changes in WC	–595	–835	730	–458
Free cash flow	196.4	–676.6	–1,798.2	413.8
WACC	9.65%	9.65%	9.65%	9.65%
Present value free cash flow	179.1	–562.7	–1,364.0	286.3

The total discounted cash flow for years 2010–2013 is:

$$179.1 - 562.7 - 1,364 + 286.3 = -€1,461.3m$$

Step 3 Estimating free cash flow for hypergrowth period

As previously observed, companies rarely go directly from high growth to constant long-term growth. In between, there is often a period of several years with a relatively high growth rate, which needs to be treated separately from the terminal value calculation. When estimating free cash flow (FCF) from these years we do not forecast each item such as EBIT, changes in working capital, etc. separately but instead forecast the free cash flow directly.

From 2014 until 2018 we estimate a constant growth rate of 8 per cent for Mobitronics' free cash flow, as we believe that added products and services in the third generation of mobile networks will increase the revenue per customer and hence growth and that all major investments have been taken coming into 2014. Note, however, that the major investments in 2010–2013 strongly influence the FCF figures for these years. In 2014, the investment period is, as noted earlier, over. Thus, when estimating FCF for 2014, we start out by assuming that the *gross cash flow* will grow by 8 per cent in 2014, but then adjust capital expenditures to the new 'normal' level of investments, by lowering it to an assumed long-term level of 46.3 per cent of EBIT, based on historical figures, as follows:

$$\text{gross cash flow 2014} = \text{gross cash flow 2013} \times (1 + g2014)$$
$$= 2{,}217.8 \times 1.08 = 2{,}395$$
$$\text{capital expenditure 2014} = \text{normalized levels of investments} \times \text{EBIT2013} \times (1 + g2014)$$
$$= 0.463 \times 1{,}911 \times 1.08 = 955.5$$
$$\text{change in WC2014} = \text{change in WC2013} \times (1 + g2014)$$
$$= 458 \times 1.08 = 494.6$$
$$\text{FCF2014} = \text{gross cash flow 2014} - \text{capital expenditure 2014} - \text{changes in WC2014}$$
$$= 2{,}395 - 955.5 - 494.6 = 945 \ (€m)$$

The above calculation is only needed for the first year of the hypergrowth period. Calculation of growth for the above-normal growth period, 2014–2018, is shown in Table 8.8. Note that each year's cash flow is discounted with WACC powered by the number of years to the present. The present value of all five years' cash flow is €2,893m.

Table 8.8 : Calculation for the above-normal growth period, 2014–2018

Year	2014	2015	2016	2017	2018	Total
Growth in free cash flow	8%	8%	8%	8%	8%	
Free cash flow	945	1,021	1,102	1,190	1,286	
WACC	9.65%	9.65%	9.65%	9.65%	9.65%	
Discount factor*	63%	58%	52%	48%	44%	
Present value of free cash flow	596	587	578	570	561	2,893

*$1/((1 + \text{WACC})^n)$

Step 4 Estimating terminal value

Determine the constant growth in free cash flow from year nine (2019) and onwards

The analysis of the business and the industry of Mobitronics is obviously extremely important for calculating the long-term growth in the company's free cash flow. What trends will the company and its sector follow from 2019 and onwards? Naturally, this analysis is by its very nature very difficult to do. However, as mentioned earlier, since long-term growth in free cash flow has a considerable impact on the terminal value and the terminal value often represents 70–80 per cent of the company's valuation, it is worth taking the time to try to make the forecasts as qualified and as well-founded as possible. Keep in mind that when calculating the terminal value we make three important assumptions, namely that Mobitronics will from 2019 to infinity:

- earn constant margins;
- grow at a constant rate;
- earn a constant return on all new investments.

If these three assumptions cannot be made, one has to extend the explicit period or the hypergrowth period until it is reasonable to believe that the assumptions hold.

As mentioned earlier, a company's growth can rarely be expected to grow faster than the economy in general over the long term. General GDP growth, industry growth and company-specific growth need to converge at some point, which is in theory in the first year of the terminal value period. The fundamental analysis performed earlier on the seven key value drivers leads us to believe that growth in EBIT will have the effect that, from year 2019 onwards, cash flows will increase at a rate of 5 per cent. This means that we believe that Mobitronics will have a growth slightly over the forecasted sector average and in the higher range of expected nominal growth in the economy in general.

This analysis is based on Mobitronics' benefiting from a mega trend of migration towards a more mobile world. Adding to this is the company's position in the market, its customer stock, its current and potential products and services, and its business model, which is not dependent on key personnel. By charting Mobitronics on a couple of current and future temporary monopoly diagrams, it becomes apparent that the company's position is very attractive. The charting suggests an ability to keep and strengthen the current market position while also entering new markets, either abroad or with new products in its home market. In short, Mobitronics should be able to further capitalize on its market position.

Calculate the terminal value

Calculate the terminal value using the terminal value formula as follows:

$$\text{Terminal value} = \frac{FCF_{n+1}}{WACC - g}$$

where FCF_{n+1} = the level of free cash flow in the first year after the explicit forecast period (here: year 2019), WACC is the weighted average cost of capital and g is the expected growth rate in free cash flow in perpetuity.

Since the terminal value is computed at year 2019, it needs to be discounted back until today. For Mobitronics we use the cash flow for the last year of the period of above-normal growth, €1,286m, and multiply this by one plus the estimated long-term constant growth of 5 per cent that begins in year 2019. This is then divided by the cost of capital of 9.65 per cent less the long-term growth for the terminal value period of 5 per cent in order to derive the terminal value. Finally, the whole amount is discounted back to the present. The calculation is as follows:

Estimation of terminal value for Mobitronics (€m) (year 2019 onwards)

$$\text{terminal value } 2018 = \frac{1,286 \times 1.05}{0.0965 - 0.05} = 29,039$$

$$\text{terminal value } 2009 = \frac{29,039}{(1 + 0.0965)^9} = 12,674 \text{ (€m)}$$

Step 5 Estimating the final DCF value of the company

Add together all discounted cash flows to receive the enterprise value

Add together the discounted cash flows from the explicit value period, the discounted value from the hypergrowth period and the discounted cash flows from the terminal value period. Then add (or deduct) all non-operating discounted cash flows (if there are any). The value achieved is called enterprise value and represents all future cash flows available to all claimants to the company.

For Mobitronics, no non-operating cash flows exist and we simply add the cash flows together:

$$\text{Mobitronics' theoretical enterprise value (EV)} =$$
$$-1{,}461 + 2{,}893 + 12{,}674 = 14{,}106 \text{ (€m)}$$

Deduct the market value of debt to receive equity value

Thereafter, the market value of the company's liabilities, minority interests and pension provisions and other claims is subtracted from the enterprise value. This gives the value of the shareholders' equity, i.e. the capital that belongs to the company's shareholders, also called market value (MV) or equity value.

Since Mobitronics has no minority interests or any pension provisions or other claims, we simply subtract the market value of the debt from the enterprise value:

$$\text{Mobitronics' equity value} = 14{,}106 - 245 = 13{,}861 \text{ (€m)}$$

Hence, the theoretical equity value of Mobitronics is €13,861 mn.

The theoretical price per share

If you want the theoretical value per share based on DCF, divide the value of the equity by the number of shares outstanding. Mobitronics has a total of 409,692,300 outstanding shares giving:

$$\text{Mobitronics' theoretical price per share} = \frac{13{,}861{,}000{,}000}{409{,}692{,}300} = 33.8 \text{ (€)}$$

According to our valuation and to the assumptions we have made, the theoretical value per share is €33.8. Currently, the share is trading at €40, implying a price per share significantly above our theoretical price per share. This concludes the DCF valuation of Mobitronics and we can summarize the valuation as shown in Table 8.9.

Table 8.9: DCF valuation of Mobitronics in summary (2009)

Weighted average cost of capital	9.65%
Present value of cash flows from explicit period	−1,461
Present value of cash flow from hypergrowth period	2,893
Present value of cash flow from terminal value period	12,674
Discounted non-operating cash flows	0
Present value of all cash flow – enterprise value	14,106
Debt (at market value)	245
Value of equity	13,861
Number of Mobitronics' shares	409,692,300
Theoretical value per Mobitronics' share	€33.8
Current market value per share	€40

Amounts in €m, except where shown otherwise.

Scenario analysis

Usually it makes sense to do a so-called scenario analysis when using a DCF valuation approach. Since all corporate value depends on future cash flows and the future is uncertain, it can be beneficial to carry out at least two other valuation scenarios added to the base-case scenario. Usually, a more optimistic scenario is postulated regarding the company's and the industry's future potential (high-case scenario) and the other scenario is less optimistic (low-case scenario). Since the terminal value is of such immense importance to overall corporate value, and the terminal value is the most difficult to estimate, it is in this calculation where the need for scenario analysis is greatest. With a starting point in financial forecasts done by the company, we feel quite comfortable with the assumptions being made in the explicit and hypergrowth period and hence we focus on elaborating on the assumptions in the terminal value period.

In our high-case scenario for Mobitronics, we have the following key terminal value assumptions (in €m):

Cost of equity	Cost of debt	WACC
11.8%	6.5%	9.65%
FCF_{n+1}	D/E ratio	g
1,350	0.42	6%

Using these assumptions in the terminal value calculations results in the following outcome (in €m):

Present value of free cash flow from terminal value	16,142
Present value of all cash flow = enterprise value	17,574
Value of equity	17,329
Theoretical value per share	42.3

In our low-case scenario, we use these terminal value assumptions (in €m):

Cost of equity	Cost of debt	WACC
11.8%	6.5%	9.65%
FCF_{n+1}	D/E ratio	g
1,200	0.42	4.5%

which gives rise to the following result (in €m):

Present value of free cash flow from terminal value	10,169
Present value of all cash flow = enterprise value	11,601
Value of equity	11,356
Theoretical value per share	27.7

Checking the underlying assumptions

It is important not only to estimate carefully the assumptions but also to check the reasonability of the assumptions made. For this we use the framework presented earlier (page 94). This will help us to analyze what our DCF assumptions imply in terms of other critical financial ratios. Assumptions made or implied for the base-case DCF valuation for Mobitronics are shown in Table 8.10.

These assumptions can now be checked using the fact that under certain assumptions, the DCF model is consistent with a number of other financial models and financial ratios. We focus only on our DCF assumptions regarding the terminal value period and analyze the long-term equilibrium ratios implied by these assumptions. In other words, we disregard all assumptions and implications regarding the period before 2019. It may appear odd to focus only on the terminal value period, but as mentioned earlier and as we saw in our earlier valuation of Mobitronics, the majority of the enterprise value often originates from this period.

Table 8.10 Explicit and implicit assumptions for base-case DCF valuation (in €m)

Cost of equity (C_E)	Cost of debt (C_D)	WACC	
11.8%	6.5%	9.65%	
Investment (Invest)	Perpetual growth in FCF (g)	Free cash flow level for terminal value (FCF_{n+1})	
1,638	5%	1,350	
Debt/equity ratio	Value of debt (MD)	Tax rate (T)	Value of equity (MV)
0.42	245	30%	13,861

We already have all variables needed for this analysis except one – invested capital – which we need to calculate. As mentioned earlier, we believe it is reasonable that due to economies of scale and large investments in new infrastructure up to 2012–2013, invested capital needed for a certain level of EBIT will decrease thereafter. Therefore, we think it is reasonable to base our calculation on invested capital in the last year of the hypergrowth period where we estimated long-term invested capital to be 46.3% of EBIT. Part of the increase in FCF during the high growth period between 2014 and 2018 was due to decreased investments in relation to EBIT. Hence, when estimating level of investment for the last year in the hypergrowth period 2018, we multiply the forecasted investment in 2014 by the growth rate of 8 per cent until 2018:

$$\text{forecast invested capital 2018} = \text{capital expenditure 2018}$$
$$= 955.5 \times 1.08^5 = 1,404$$

We will now check our explicit and implicit DCF assumptions using some of the most common ratios – return on capital (ROC), return on equity (ROE), price to earnings ratio (P/E) and price to book value (P/B).

Implied return on capital (ROC)

First, we are interested in reviewing what ROC our DCF assumptions imply. ROC is calculated as:

$$\text{ROC} = \frac{\text{NOPAT} \times g}{\text{invest}}$$

where NOPAT is long-term net operating profit after taxes in the first year of the terminal value period and invest is new investment needed for this level of NOPAT, i.e. forecasted investment for 2019.

$$\text{FCF 2019} = 1{,}286 \times 1.05 = 1{,}350$$
$$\text{investments 2019} = 1{,}404 \times 1.05 = 1{,}474$$

For Mobitronics, we calculate NOPAT as:

$$\text{NOPAT} = \text{FCF 2019} + \text{invest 2019} = 1{,}350 + 1{,}474 = 2{,}824$$

With NOPAT being 2,824 and growth and investments already given, we calculate ROC for Mobitronics as follows:

$$\frac{2{,}824 \times 0.05}{1{,}474} = 0.0958$$

That Mobitronics should be able to give 9.58 per cent ROC in the long run, considering that its cost of capital is 9.65 per cent, seems like a modest estimate since it, in fact, implies capital destruction (ROC below the cost of capital). It is, however, no cause for panic; as long as the ratios do not differ more than in this example, it does not motivate a revaluation but can instead be viewed as an argument as to why the valuation is conservative.

Some academics argue that it is highly unlikely that any company will be able to maintain a ROC over its cost of capital in the long run and that it will always dwindle towards zero. Therefore, this is a very important and valuable checkpoint for your valuation. If your DCF valuation implies a long-term return on capital significantly higher than the company's cost of capital, it is likely to be too aggressive and you should probably rework your terminal value assumptions and valuation or be ready to argue your case. If it differs slightly, you do not have to redo the valuation but can instead use it as part of your overall view of the valuation as aggressive, moderate or conservative.

Implied return on equity (ROE)

We move on to ROE, which is calculated as:

$$ROE = \frac{g}{1 - P}$$

where g is long-term growth in free cash flow and P is the payout ratio calculated as P = dividends/earnings. In order to calculate the payout ratio we then need dividends and earnings, which we calculate as:

$$Dividends = FCF + new\ debt - interest\ payments\ (post\text{-}tax)$$

where

$$New\ debt = market\ value\ of\ debt \times g$$

and

$$Interest\ payments\ (post\text{-}tax) = MD \times C_D \times (1 - T)$$

where

$$MD = long\text{-}term\ market\ value\ of\ debt\ defined\ as\ EV \times \frac{D}{D + E}$$

where EV = enterprise value from the DCF calculation, and D/(D + E) = debt in relation to total capital, C_D = cost of debt and T = tax rate. Earnings is then simply calculated as:

$$Earnings = dividends + invest - new\ debt$$

For Mobitronics, we start by calculating debt in relation to total capital, market value of debt, interest payments (post-tax), new debt and dividends. Debt in relation to total capital is calculated as earlier: if D/E = 0.42 then E/D = 1/(D/E) and 1/0.42 = 2.38. From that it follows that D/(D + E) = 1/(1 + 2.38) = 0.2958 = 29.58 per cent.

$$\text{long-term market value of debt} = EV \times \frac{D}{D + E}$$

$$= 14{,}106 \times 0.2958 = 4{,}173$$

$$\text{interest payments} = MD \times C_D \times (1 - T)$$

$$= 4{,}173 \times 0.065 \times (1 - 0.3) = 189.8$$

$$\text{new debt} = \text{market value of debt} \times g$$

$$= 4{,}173 \times 0.05 = 208.65$$

$$\text{dividends} = \text{FCF 2019} + \text{new debt} - \text{interest payments (post tax)}$$

$$= 1{,}350 + 208.65 - 189.8 = 1{,}368.85$$

With dividends, earnings are easily calculated as:

$$\text{earnings} = \text{dividends} + \text{invest} - \text{new debt}$$

$$= 1{,}368.85 + 1{,}474 - 208.65 = 2{,}634.2$$

With earnings and dividends in place, the payout ratio is:

$$\text{payout ratio} = \frac{\text{dividends}}{\text{earnings}}$$

$$= \frac{1{,}368.85}{2{,}634.2} = 0.5196$$

And finally we reach an ROE calculation of

$$ROE = \frac{0.05}{1 - 0.5196} = 0.1041 = 10.41\%$$

Similarly to the return on capital, ROE can be used as a checkpoint for your DCF valuation as many academics argue that in the long run ROE will converge with the company's cost of equity.

For Mobitronics, a ROE of 10.41 per cent may seem low since the estimated cost of equity is 11.8 per cent. Similarly to the ROC discussion earlier, a long-term ROE below its cost of equity indicates that in the long run Mobitronics will be destroying value (since only ROE over its cost of equity will create value). In practice, this suggests that as soon as Mobitronics no longer generates returns over its cost of equity, the company should be liquidated and the assets returned to the shareholders. Of course, another possibility is that our DCF terminal value assumptions were too modest and need to be made more aggressive.

Implied price to earnings (P/E)

The price to earnings ratio is calculated as:

$$\text{Price/earnings} = \frac{P}{C_E - g}$$

where P = the payout ratio, C_E is the cost of equity and g is the long-term growth rate.

Since C_E and g were given from our DCF valuation and we have already calculated the payout ratio we just insert the numbers:

$$\text{price/earnings} = \frac{0.5196}{0.118 - 0.05} = 7.64$$

Similarly to our ROC and ROE checks, the implied long-term P/E ratio of 7.64 may appear low. Considering that the company is currently trading at a P/E of 18 and that the industry average is slightly lower at 16.5, a 7.64 P/E ratio in the long run could perhaps indicate that our DCF long-term assumptions are too modest. However, as the growth in the terminal value period is lower than the current growth, long-term P/E should in fact be lower than the current.

Implied price to book value

The price to book (P/B) value places the value of the company in relation to the value of the company's equity in its balance sheet. It can be calculated as:

$$\text{Price/book} = \text{price/earnings} \times \text{ROE}$$

Since we have already calculated both P/E and ROE, it is an easy task to compute long-term P/B:

$$\text{price/book} = 7.64 \times 0.1041 = 0.795$$

As mentioned in Chapter 4, P/B is not a suitable ratio for most companies, especially not growth companies such as Mobitronics. However, an implied P/B of 0.795 could indicate that the long-term assumptions for the DCF valuations are low since Mobitronics will be valued at a 20% discount to its book value.

Multiple-based valuation of Mobitronics

We have now conducted a full DCF valuation of Mobitronics and checked the underlying assumptions for reasonableness. A different and complementary approach to valuing Mobitronics would be to use fundamental and/or relative multiples to estimate the value of the company. As mentioned in previous chapters, multiple valuations can be used as a way to quickly get a rough valuation estimate for a company to see if it is worthwhile to engage in more complex valuations, such as a DCF analysis. Alternatively, it can be done to complement a standalone valuation model, such as a DCF model, to check the reasonableness of the final valuation results. Also, multiples are easy to compare and discuss, and therefore it is usually worthwhile to spend some time analyzing some of the most important multiples. Finally, relative multiples give an estimate of how the public market would value the company, which for more short-term investments might be of the greatest importance.

The multiples implied by the DCF valuation in the previous section were based on expected long-term equilibrium values since they were derived from the terminal value assumptions in the DCF model. Equilibrium multiples are generally best suited for checking assumptions from a standalone valuation model such as the DCF model. For the purpose of valuing a business therefore, it is common to use current or next year's forecasted financial data as a basis for multiple valuations. These forecasts are generally available for public companies and normally reasonably accurate. In theory, one wants to use the data that are consistent with the long-term financial trend and if next year's financials are not consistent with the long term, then one is usually better off using another year's financial data or trend historical data.

For the three multiples we have chosen – price/sales, EV/EBITDA and price/earnings – we will calculate both the fundamental and the relative multiple. Regarding Mobitronics' financial data, we assess that next year's (2010) financials are a good estimate of trends in sales, EBITDA and earnings and will therefore use those data to calculate the multiples.

EV/Price/sales

First, we start by calculating the sales multiple, based on current financial fundamentals. Since the formula for the fundamental P/S multiple includes the payout ratio (how much of the profit the shareholders get), it transforms an enterprise flow to all claimants to an equity flow only available to shareholders. Therefore, we can use the P/S multiple instead of the EV/S multiple. The general formula for price/sales is:

$$\text{Price/sales} = \text{profit margin} \times \text{payout ratio} \times \frac{1+g}{C_E - g}$$

where profit margin is defined as earnings/revenues, payout ratio is dividend/earnings, g is long-term growth rate in dividends and earnings, and C_E is cost of equity.

For Mobitronics, all data are directly available from earlier calculations, except for the profit margin, which we calculate as:

$$\text{forecast profit margin 2010} = \frac{1{,}236}{5{,}313} = 0.2326 = 23.26\%$$

And now we calculate price/sales as follows:

$$\frac{\text{price}}{\text{sales}} = 0.2326 \times 0.5196 \times \frac{1+0.05}{0.118 - 0.05} = 1.87$$

Based on Mobitronics' fundamentals, the stock should theoretically be trading at a price/sales multiple of 1.87. If the stock is trading at a price/sales multiple over 1.87 it implies that the stock might be overvalued, and if the stock is trading at a price/sales multiple below 1.87 that it might be undervalued.

Applying the fundamental sales multiple on Mobitronics' forecast sales for next year yields the following corporate value:

$$\text{Equity value} = \text{price/sales} \times \text{forecasted sales for next year}$$

$$= 1.87 \times 5{,}313 = 9{,}935 \ (\text{€m})$$

This equity value can then be compared with the equity value received from the DCF analysis, which was €13,861m.

Instead of calculating the price/sales based on the fundamental financials of Mobitronics, one could instead use the price/sales multiple of a traded company with similar characteristics to Mobitronics, or, alternatively, use an industry average to calculate the relative multiple.

For Mobitronics, we assess that it is most reasonable to apply the industry average since the peer group is relatively homogenous but no single competitor has such similar characteristics as to warrant a direct comparison. The current average price/sales multiple for mobile operators is 2. Applying the industry average price/sales multiple to Mobitronics' sales gives:

$$\text{equity value} = 2 \times 5{,}313 = 10{,}626 \ (\text{€m})$$

This valuation too can then be compared to the DCF valuation or any other valuation.

Obviously, as discussed in Chapter 5, a relative valuation based only on sales is very rough since it, for example, leaves the company-specific cost structure completely out of the valuation.

EV/EBITDA

Second, we calculate the multiple most used by valuation professionals, EV/EBITDA. The general formula is:

$$\text{EV/EBITDA} = \frac{\text{ROIC} - g}{\text{ROIC} \times (\text{WACC} - g)} \times (1 - T) \times (1 - DA)$$

where ROIC is return on invested capital, g is long-term growth rate, WACC is weighted average cost of capital, T is the tax rate and DA is depreciation and amortization as a percentage of EBITDA.

We calculate ROIC as:

$$\text{ROIC} = \frac{\text{NOPLAT}}{\text{invested capital}}$$

where invested capital is calculated as:

> Invested capital
>
> = all operating working capital invested in the company
>
> + net fixed assets + other assets net of other liabilities

and NOPLAT is calculated as:

> NOPLAT = EBIT – cash taxes on EBIT

For Mobitronics, using forecasted financials for 2010 yields:

$$\text{invested capital } 2010 = (937 + 818 - 1{,}232) + 3{,}224 = 3{,}747$$

$$\text{NOPLAT } 2010 = 1{,}746 - 501.6 = 1{,}244.4$$

which gives:

$$\text{ROIC } 2010 = \frac{1{,}244.4}{3{,}747} = 0.332$$

Now we need to divide forecasted depreciation and amortization by EBITDA.

$$\text{DA} = \frac{542}{2{,}288} = 0.2369$$

$$\text{EV/EBITDA} = \frac{0.332 - 0.05}{0.332 \times (0.0965 - 0.05)} \times 0.7 \times 0.7631 = 9.76$$

Considering that the industry average EV/EBITDA is 7, and that Mobitronics is currently trading at an EV/EBITDA multiple of 7.16, this multiple seems quite high. This may be due to significant fluctuations of this year's EBITDA and/or that the market significantly values Mobitronics lower than its fundamentals warrant.

Applying the multiple to the forecasted EBITDA for 2010 gives the following calculation:

$$\text{EV} = \text{EV/EBITDA} \times \text{EBITDA} = 9.76 \times 2{,}288 = 22{,}325 \ (\text{€m})$$

and an equity value of:

$$22,325 - 245 = 22,080 \text{ (€m)}$$

The reason for the high EV/EBITDA multiple is that the ROIC for 2010 is 33.2 per cent. As mentioned, a deviant multiple might be due to yearly fluctuations. The question then becomes whether the ROIC for 2010 is representative also for future years. Looking at 2011 and 2012, however, reveals that invested capital is forecasted to increase significantly more than NOPLAT. In 2011, NOPLAT is expected to increase by 4.3 per cent (from €1,244.4m to €1,298.4m) while invested capital is forecasted to increase by 52 per cent (from €3,747m to €5,722m). We therefore calculate ROIC for 2011:

$$\text{ROIC 2011} = \frac{1,298.4}{5,722} = 22.7\%$$

An analysis of the forecasted income statement and balance sheet for 2012, 2013, etc. shows that 2011, and the ROIC for 2011, is more representative for the long-term development of the company than the equivalent 2010 figures. Therefore, we also calculate EV/EBITDA using 2011 figures.

$$\text{EV/EBITDA} = \frac{0.227 - 0.05}{0.227 \times (0.0965 - 0.05)} \times 0.7 \times 0.7307 = 8.57$$

This results in an EV/EBITDA ratio slightly above the industry average but more reasonable as a long-term multiple than the 2010 figure.

Applying the multiple on 2010 EBITDA gives:

$$\text{EV} = 8.57 \times 2,288 = 19,608 \text{ (€m)}$$

and an equity value of:

$$19,608 - 245 = 19,363 \text{ (€m)}$$

This value can, of course, be compared with the value received from the DCF valuation carried out earlier of €13,861m and we can conclude that the DCF valuation gave a value significantly lower than the valuation based on the EV/EBITDA calculation. Also, one can instead apply EV/EBITDA for a similar company or the industry average to Mobitronics' earnings. The industry average EV/EBITDA multiple is 7 and applying that relative multiple to Mobitronics' forecasted EBITDA for 2010 gives:

$$EV = EV/EBITDA \times EBITDA = 7 \times 2,288 = 16,016 \ (€m)$$

and an equity value of:

$$16,016 - 245 = 15,771 \ (€m)$$

The above analysis shows that the multiple valuations seem to give a value significantly above our DCF valuation, which seems to be more conservative than both the relative and fundamental multiple valuations. Again, this does not have to be cause for action but gives you additional input to any discussion regarding the value of the company and to your investment or divestment decision.

EV/capacity or revenue-generating units

Finally, we want to use an operational variable to calculate company value and compare with the competitors in the industry. For Mobitronics, we believe that the most suitable operational variable to use is its subscription base, i.e. its customers. This is because the forecasted growth will come mainly from increasing revenue per customer as explained in Chapter 6, which in turn connects closely to growth in cash flow (and therefore value). Consequently, we will use EV/customer as our operational multiple. Certainly, for other companies and industries the variables will be completely different. In those cases, one simply exchanges customer for a different operational variable.

Fundamentally, EV/customer can be calculated as:

$$EV/customer = \frac{ROIC - g}{ROIC \times (WACC - g)} \times \frac{NOPAT}{customer}$$

The only figure we do not have is NOPAT per customer. Using NOPAT (and ROIC) for 2011, since we found earlier that it is more representative of future development, and dividing by Mobitronics' current number of customers gives:

$$\frac{NOPLAT \ 2011}{number \ of \ customers} = \frac{1,248,000,000}{9,130,000} = 137$$

Using ROIC for 2011 (since the ROIC during 2011 is more representative for future development) gives:

$$\text{EV/customer} = \frac{0.227 - 0.05}{0.227 \times (0.965 - 0.05)} \times 137 = 2{,}297$$

Multiplying EV/customer by the number of customers yields an enterprise value of €20,972m and an equity value of €20,727m. Comparing the EV/customer for Mobitronics with other companies in the industry shows that all other companies have a slightly lower value per customer. This appears reasonable as Mobitronics is more focused on the business segment, provides more services to its customers and has revenue per customer that outstrips the competitors.

Considering the fact that all other competitors in the industry have a lower EV/customer than Mobitronics, it follows that the value of Mobitronics will be too low using a competitor's EV/customer or the industry average. It can, however, be interesting to view how much the value of Mobitronics theoretically would fall if the revenue per customer should fall to industry average levels. Using the industry average of 1500 gives:

$$\text{EV} = \text{EV/customer} \times \text{no. of customers} = 1{,}500 \times 9{,}130{,}000 = 13{,}695 \ (\text{€m})$$

giving an equity value of

$$= 13{,}695 - 245 = 13{,}450 \ (\text{€m})$$

Piecing it all together – the value of the company

Based on the rather comprehensive analysis above, we now have the following inputs for a valuation discussion (€m):

DCF valuation	Valuation	Implied ROC spread	Implied ROE spread	Implied P/E
Low case	11,356	8.21% – 9.65% = –1.44%	8.56% – 11.8% = –3.22%	6.51
Base case	13,861	9.58% – 9.65% = –0.07%	10.41% – 11.8% = –1.39%	7.64
High case	17,329	10.94% – 9.65% = 1.29%	11.4% – 11.8% = –0.4%	8.20

Multiples	Fundamental equity value	Relative equity value
P/sales	9,935	10,626
EV/EBITDA (2011)	19,363	15,771
EV/customer	20,727	13,450

Displaying the result of the different valuation approaches graphically gives us Figure 8.2.

Comparing the different valuation methods, we can conclude that the DCF low-case scenario may be too conservative when checking the implied assumptions. As we could see in our analysis of the base-case DCF assumptions, the implied ROC and ROE were lower than their respective cost of capital. The high-case scenario, on the other hand, results in a ROC higher than the cost of capital but still a ROE lower than the cost

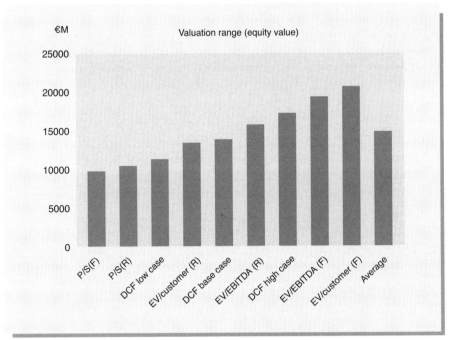

FIGURE 8.2   Valuation of Mobitronics – comparing the different valuation approaches

of equity. This, together with the EV/EBITDA multiple estimate and the EV/customer multiple estimate, leads us to believe that a value around our high-case scenario between €17,000m and €18,000m seems most likely to be a fair estimate. This would also result in ROC and ROE spreads that possibly could be defended as sustainable in the long term. This implies a value per share between €41.5 and €43.9.

Summary

In this chapter, we have completed a full valuation of our model company, Mobitronics. We went through the following key steps:

- **Underlying analysis of Mobitronics,** where we used the framework presented in Chapter 7 to analyze the intellectual capital within Mobitronics and the industry structure surrounding the company. We focused our analysis around the seven key variables: brand strength, management and board motivation and past performance, innovation power, person-independent knowledge, sector growth, relative market share and entry barriers.

- **DCF valuation of Mobitronics,** where, based on the underlying analysis and historical financial data, we forecasted free cash flows, growth in free cash flows, and cost of capital for the explicit period, the hypergrowth period and the terminal period. We then discounted all future cash flow streams, added them together and deducted market value of debt to arrive at a theoretical equity value of Mobitronics of €13,861m and a theoretical value per share of €33.8.

- **Scenario analysis,** conducted by altering some of the key input variables in the DCF analysis such as cost of capital, capital structure and long-term free cash flow growth. In our high-case scenario we arrived at a theoretical equity value of Mobitronics of €17,329m and a value per share of €42. In the low-case scenario, we arrived at a total equity value of €11,356m and a value per share of €27.7.

- **Checking the underlying assumptions,** where we used the mathematical relationships between various key valuation models to view implicitly assumed financial ratios. We saw that our base-case DCF assumptions implicitly assumed a return on capital (ROC) of 9.58 per cent and a return on equity (ROE) of 10.41 per cent. Considering that Mobitronics has a cost of capital of 9.65 per cent and a cost of equity of 11.8 per cent and the resulting implicit long-term P/E ratio of 7.64, we concluded that our DCF assumptions may seem too modest.

■ **Multiple-based valuation of the company**, where we used funda-mental and relative sales, EBITDA and operational ratios to estimate the value of Mobitronics. According to the ratios, the equity value is between €9,935m and €20,727m, depending on the multiple used.

Finally, we put everything together and argued that according to our anal-ysis a fair estimation of the value of Mobitronics lies somewhere between €17,000m and €18,000m, implying a theoretical value per share between €41.5 and €43.9.

In our final chapter, we will be taking a closer look at value-based manage-ment (VBM).

9

Value-based management

What topics are covered in this chapter?

- Strategy development
- Target setting
- Action plans, budgets and training
- Incentive programmes
- Outcomes of value-based management
- Summary

Value-based management is a practical operational application of the concepts and frameworks presented earlier in this book. Consequently, this chapter is mostly aimed towards people with an interest in managerial issues, including executives, board members, entrepreneurs, etc.

As we have argued earlier in the book, the first step towards maximizing the value of a company is to understand how to measure and calculate its value accurately. Furthermore, the financial valuation is completely dependent on the input variables and hence the company's key value drivers need to be analyzed. Let us now move on to a discussion regarding how to implement these theories in a managerial context.

Value-based management (VBM) is a management approach focused on maximizing corporate value and prioritizing decisions according to how those decisions affect overall corporate value.

The basic concept is the transformation of DCF, EVA and other similar valuation models into a management tool for making major strategic as well as everyday operating decisions. In VBM you ask, 'How should we manage our company in order to receive the highest possible future cash flows, and therefore highest value?' It might sound like a concept only for top management, but VBM is, in fact, applicable at all levels of an organization.

Perhaps the two most concrete differences apparent when using VBM instead of pure income statement based management and measurement techniques are that:

▪ **VBM requires managing the balance sheet as well as the income statement**. A well-managed balance sheet is generally not required when a company, its departments and its individuals are measured solely on the last period's financial statement, e.g. net income. As we explained in Chapter 6, the increase/decrease in capital employed in inventories, customer accounts, etc. also affects cash flow and thus value. Since VBM strives to maximize the value of a company, it requires attention to the balance sheet as well as to the income statement.

▪ **VBM requires a long-term perspective**. In today's fast-moving financial markets, companies are often focused on the result for the next quarter, since they wish to live up to the demands of the stock market and its analysts. In addition, many companies have quarterly based incentive programmes. This, of course, makes the focus short-term for managers and employees, resulting in decisions that might not be value-maximizing in the long run. A large number of examples exist where management rejected long-term profitable projects because of negative short-term effects. Since VBM takes a long-term approach, it aids in balancing long-term with short-term perspectives.

One can divide VBM and its implementation into four distinct processes that are all necessary in order to receive the full benefits from VBM:

1 Strategy development
2 Target setting
3 Action plans/budgeting
4 Incentive systems.

Strategy development

In order to maximize the company's value, the board and management must decide on which strategy to employ. This decision includes which business the company should be in and which it should not be in, and hence which subsidiaries/departments it should divest and which it will prioritize. It also needs to decide whether it should employ a growth strategy and try to increase market share, perhaps accepting the decrease in short-term cash flow, or a harvest strategy focusing on maximizing short-term cash flow.

When analyzing the different options, a functional approach is to calculate the expected value of future cash flows from the different available strategies using relevant key ratio assumptions. As always, it is difficult to forecast many of the input variables for the different strategies correctly, but an analysis of this sort will at least allow you to compare the sensitivity of the different strategies with certain key assumptions.

It is important to corroborate key assumptions and key value driver projections with top mangement when analyzing different business unit strategies

Once the overall corporate strategy is set, business unit managers need to review different strategies for their business units and align them to the overall corporate strategy, while at the same time maximizing business unit value. It is important to corroborate key assumptions and key value driver projections with top management when analyzing different business unit strategies. Here again, scenario analysis can be most beneficial in estimating how the strategic decisions are affected by differing assumptions.

Target setting

After the overall company strategy and business units' strategies to maximize corporate value are in place, they must be transformed into specific and concrete short- and long-term objectives. Without these concretely specified goals, the people in the organization will not know what variables to focus on. It is important to put substantial effort into determining reasonable targets. Some guidelines are:

▨ Include both financial and non-financial targets. The combination ensures that management will not sacrifice investments in important areas, essential in the long run, in order to reach short-term financial goals. In addition, financial targets measure what has happened historically, whereas non-financial targets often measure what is about to happen. If, for example, customer retention or sales from new products have fallen, then this could be considered a warning sign that customer service or product quality is not good enough or that the company's product range might soon be outdated.

◼ Include both short-term and long-term targets. This prevents management from focusing on short-term gains that might not be optimal in the long run. It is, of course, of utmost importance that the long-term and short-term targets are compatible.

◼ Adapt the targets for different levels in the organization; top management needs a different type of target than that for R&D personnel or customer support.

For financial long-term target setting, the reader should not be too surprised when we strongly believe that corporate value, the discounted value of all future cash flows, is the only appropriate measure. However, as a measurement in the short term, corporate value as predicted in a DCF model can be difficult to use – at least since it involves a large number of predictions of future cash flow and does not give any appropriate measurements for short-term financial performance. Therefore, one needs an additional measurement for short-term financial performance such as economic profit or economic value added (EVA).

Economic profit is tightly linked to value and is the marginal added value (or subtracted value) to a company's total value for a specific period. A similar measurement for short-term and periodic financial performance is EVA, which we presented earlier in Chapter 4. EVA can be explained as a fine-tuned economic profit and is usually expressed as:

EVA = (ROIC − WACC) × invested capital at the beginning of the year

By analyzing the EVA formula, we can conclude that the management needs to do any of the following to increase EVA and hence value:

1 Increase ROIC while holding WACC and the invested capital constant.

2 Decrease WACC while holding ROIC and invested capital constant. Usually, corporate managers finance their companies with too much equity, wanting to minimize the financial risk of the business. VBM and EVA encourage managers to focus also on the cost of capital. Experience shows that as managers are motivated to improve the capital structure, it usually results in the company acquiring more debt and adopting a more aggressive capital structure.

3 Increase the invested capital in projects/activities yielding a ROIC greater than WACC.

4 Withdraw capital from projects/activities that yield a ROIC lower than WACC. This might mean selling divisions or subsidiaries that do not produce over cost of capital returns.

5 Have longer periods where the company is expected to earn a ROIC greater than WACC.

An incentive system based solely on EVA or economic profit can be counter-productive and therefore needs to be combined with other long-term measurements

The problem with using only economic profit or only EVA is the possibility of generating incorrect short-term incentives. This is because in a particular project, EVA or economic profit might be negative in the first few years of the project but have a positive net present value in total and thereby create shareholder value. If you base an incentive plan on EVA or economic profit alone, it might mean that even though a project is progressing according to plan and is creating shareholder value, the employee will receive no compensation in the first few years as the project has a negative short-term value added. Consequently, if an employee has a time horizon shorter than the lifetime of the project, he or she might reject the project, even though it creates shareholder value. Hence, an incentive system based solely on EVA or economic profit can be counter-productive and therefore needs to be combined with other long-term measurements.

In terms of non-financial objectives, the overall goal of maximizing future cash flow and corporate value must be transformed into concrete non-financial key variables. Though non-financial key value drivers vary from industry to industry and company to company, generic non-financial key variables exist as well, as was shown in Chapter 7. It is important that the chosen key non-financial variables are linked closely to the creation of value. If not, one might instead destroy value. In addition, key value drivers are not static and will probably change over time and it will therefore be necessary to review them periodically.

Action plans, budgets and training

When the company has short- and long-term financial and non-financial targets in place, it is time to map a step-by-step action plan to achieve these goals. Since it is often easier for employees further down in the organization to relate to other objectives than purely financial ones, it is important not only to express action plans and budgets in financial terms but also to connect these plans to operational measures.

However, these targets should, of course, be connected to value creation. For example, use a ROIC tree as shown in Figure 9.1 to derive the necessary operational variables to use as targets. Also, experience has shown

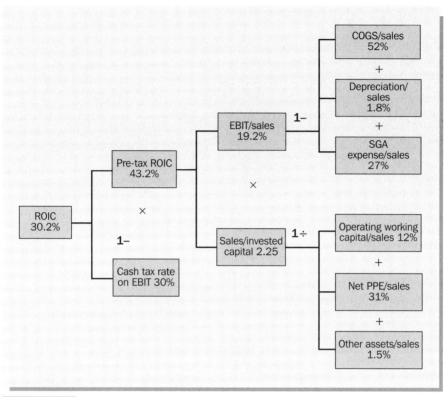

FIGURE 9.1 ROIC value tree

that it is important to devote time to designing a training programme for the value creation process in the company. The aim of the training programme should be to commit the organization to VBM's success by achieving an understanding of the concept and why it is a good method for managing and measuring performance.

Usually, it is advisable to wait with the explanation of the new incentive plan until a later stage since compensation discussions tend to absorb more energy and focus and employees are more likely to buy into the incentive programme after having seen the VBM programme at work in reality.

Also, normally, the training should be conducted in stages with a preliminary session explaining the basic rationales behind the VBM programme, introducing the employees to the concept and why it is a useful measurement of company as well as employee performance. Later, a workshop should be designed to explore the VBM programme in more detail.

Incentive programmes

Creating an incentive system based on maximizing shareholder value is an integral part of VBM. 'What you measure and reward gets done.' In other words, if incentives are linked to net sales, focus will be on net sales, if they are linked to net result, focus will be on net result and if linked to the share price, time will be spent checking the stock quote. So, if you want to maximize the value of the corporation, you need a motivation and compensation programme that is linked to maximizing company value – for as many employees as practically possible.

Every business faces the question of how best to motivate and reward its employees in order to retain them in the company and, furthermore, to create value for the owners of the company. If the owners are not constantly to have to overview and monitor the performance and the decisions in the company, a compensation policy is needed to align employee incentives with owner incentives. This is, in essence, what a VBM incentive programme is all about. Generally, employee compensation can be divided into two parts – the base pay and a performance-based pay. Incentive programmes regulate the performance-based part of the remuneration and VBM incentive programmes are no exception.

When creating a VBM-based incentive programme, it is important (as in all incentive programmes) to use objectives that the individual, team or department has the power to influence and which are in line with their responsibilities. As mentioned, one should link incentives both to financial goals measuring the overall financial performance and value creation of the company, and to non-financial goals linked to sales, customer satisfaction, production efficiency, product quality or similar operative variables.

Generally, a VBM-based incentive programme can be designed in the following fashion:

■ Relate the top management incentives to financial objectives only. As a long-term financial objective, the DCF value of the corporation is the ultimate measure. However, as previously mentioned, as the DCF is based on forecasts and not actual results it is not suitable as a basis for incentives. The stock price, on the other hand, is heavily influenced by market conditions and sentiment that the management cannot influence. Instead, the suggestion is to use an EVA measure as a short-term valuation measurement and the stock price for longer-term incentives.

The stock-related incentives should be long-term and constructed so as to avoid stock price manipulation.

■ Business unit managers' incentives could be based on a combination of overall company financial objectives, specific business unit financial objectives and specific non-financial business unit objectives. The non-financial objectives for the business unit should, of course, be based on previously determined key value drivers. It is important that the managers feel that they can influence a major part of the set objectives. As the operating characteristics of the different business units often vary, one cannot use the same objectives. Instead, they need to be tailored to each business unit.

■ Functional managers could be rewarded mainly based on non-financial measures for their area of responsibility. For a sales manager it could mean customer retention, customer acquisitions or customer satisfaction whereas for a product development manager it could mean product development time or sales of new products developed. Complement this with a minor part of the incentive based on overall financial objectives.

Other employees are normally rewarded mainly based on the same measures as the functional managers but on an individual and/or group level and not on a business unit level. Also, non-financial incentives should be complemented with a smaller part of financial incentives related to the performance of the entire group in order to increase the focus on maximizing value.

It is important to note that the idea is to give the whole organization a performance-based incentive programme, not just the CEO or the top executives.

A shift towards value-based incentive programmes is an extremely important ingredient in a VBM programme. Without aligning employee incentives with overall company goals, a VBM programme is unlikely to be successful. In fact, to put it differently, managers will not run the company with the aim of delivering as much shareholder value as possible unless the company rewards them for it. Successfully implemented, it will affect all areas of work within the company and transform everything from work ethics to decision-making within the company.

Outcomes of value-based management

So, how well does VBM work? Since a full implementation of VBM is neither an easy nor a fast process, the benefits must be substantial in order to
justify the work during the year it usually takes to complete an implementation of VBM.

Clearly, VBM suits some companies and not others. There are certainly a
large number of success stories using VBM, but there are also examples of
companies that tried to implement VBM and then abandoned it after a
while. Specifically, VBM is far more easily implemented in a company active
in a stable industry than for a firm that operates in rapidly changing markets. In high-growth industries, the company value is usually linked closely
to the firm's future growth opportunities, which generally is much more
difficult to assess than is an ongoing operation in a more mature industry.
A few key parameters are important to consider before implementing a
VBM programme:

▪ **Allocate sufficient time for implementation**. Most companies agree
that implementing VBM requires time and patience. First, managers
and employees must learn to understand the value-maximizing process and how key value drivers link everyday tasks to overall corporate
value. Thereafter, a VBM incentive system can be installed. If the management tries to implement the incentive system before employees
understand and accept VBM, then the risk is that it will not yield the
desired results. The total process normally takes at least a year before it
starts yielding results.

▪ **Top management support is essential**. All evidence suggests that it is
of utmost importance that top management provides its full support
during the implementation of the VBM programme and that it devotes
time to the process.

▪ **Link the incentive system to VBM**. It is not recommended to use
VBM as a management tool while not using it as a basis for employee
compensation for any long period of time. An aligned incentive programme is needed in order to change organizational behaviour. Again,
what is measured and rewarded gets done. If you will not, or cannot,
implement a VBM-based incentive system, you should carefully consider not implementing any VBM system at all.

▪ **General education about VBM is crucial**. In order for VBM to be
implemented successfully and accepted, people in the organization
need to understand it. Significant investments in terms of money and

time need to be made in order to educate properly as many of the employees as practically possible. Only when employees understand VBM will it be trusted and gain support.

■ **Make it simple**. Implementing VBM is an extensive exercise and it should be simplified as much as possible. It is vital that as many as possible in the company understand the VBM programme and how the incentive programme works. Take time to ensure that the information regarding the programme is easily understood and readily available.

■ **VBM should be a company-wide programme for the daily running of the business**. The real benefits from VBM do not usually come from using it to decide whether capital investment projects should be accepted or rejected. Instead, a VBM programme makes the most difference and truly enhances value in the day-to-day running of the business in all sections of the organization.

■ **Alter the programme to suit your company profile**. Even though general guidelines can be of great help when implementing VBM, the process of implementing a VBM programme is highly specific to each company. Consequently, company-specific adaptations are always necessary.

So what are the benefits? Well, the most important benefit is that employees feel and act like shareholders and are motivated to maximize shareholder value. Secondly, almost all companies have experienced better utilization of the capital employed in the company after implementing a VBM programme. VBM forces management to identify excess costs and rethink the use of capital, resulting in decreased inventories, reduced accounts receivable, reduced cash balance or other similar measurements. Also, VBM will normally help management identify subsidiaries, departments or under-utilized assets that should be sold or otherwise disposed of in order to create shareholder value and increase employee compensation. Thirdly, as the general level of motivation increases, more beneficial relationships with customers, suppliers and other stakeholders are usually developed. Finally, it helps management to understand the interrelationship between strategy and value.

Summary

In this chapter we discussed how to put our valuation knowledge into a managerial context. A management approach focused on maximizing corporate value and prioritizing decisions according to how those decisions affect overall corporate value is called value-based management (VBM).

Generally, the implementation of a VBM programme can be divided into the following four processes:

1 **Strategy development**, where the company's strategies for maximizing corporate value are mapped out.

2 **Target setting**, where the overall strategy is transformed into specific and concrete short- and long-term objectives. It is important to include both financial and non-financial operational variables and to adapt them for all levels in the organization.

3 **Action plans/budgeting and training**, where the company's plan and budget to achieve the targets are set up.

4 **Incentive systems**, where employee incentives are linked to corporate value. It is important to use objectives that the individual, team or department has the power to influence and which are in line with their responsibilities.

An important benefit of VBM is that it requires close management of the balance sheet, not only the income statement. This means that managers have to be concerned about how they handle the capital employed in the company, for example how they manage investments, working capital, etc.

Equally important is that VBM requires a long-term perspective. Instead of giving management incentives to maximize short-term profit, VBM aligns management incentives with owner incentives – to create long-term value.

When setting up a VBM programme, it is important to make it as simple as possible and to devote significant management time to it. The concept needs to be carefully explained and employees need to be educated. It is also important that VBM is a company-wide programme, and that result requires time and patience.

Afterword

Our aspiration has been to place this book in the *must-have* category of a business professional's literature. We wrote it because we perceived a need for a concise, comprehensible, no-nonsense guide to the art of company valuations. At the same time we made sure not to write too hefty a tome (there are already far too many gathering dust on the bookshelves of would-be corporate valuation enthusiasts all over the world). We felt that a practical yet comprehensive book could add greatly to the existing literature on the subject. We sincerely hope that we have succeeded and that the reader finds the subject of valuation less mysterious and more approachable after reading this book.

We also intend the reader to use this book as a handy reference or as an introduction to the study of valuations. Note that the emphasis here is on 'handy' and, though the book discusses both the main terminology and the concepts used in corporate valuations in some depth, we encourage the ambitious reader to complement this book with other more detailed and perhaps more theoretical works.

On a final note, it is worth mentioning the authors' view of the shareholder value movement. Due to the increasing importance of and focus on the maximization of shareholder value and the creation of shareholder wealth, it is becoming more and more common to measure the performance of capital employed in a business. This in turn forces capital to be used in the most efficient way possible and will drive innovations and technological advancements as capital seeks ways to increase returns. These advancements, and the process as a whole, benefit society and increase the wealth of the world in general. Consequently, we sincerely reject the shareholder value phenomenon as something anti-humanistic and short-sighted. Instead, aspirations regarding value creation should be viewed as nothing less than aspirations for societal improvement.

We wish you all the best in your future valuations!

Jakob Tolleryd and David Frykman

Appendix A

Inspirational list of key value drivers

Financial value drivers

Average maturity of debt/average maturity of assets This measures the firm's sensitivity to changes in interest rates. The closer the ratio is to one, the less sensitive is the company. Generally, you want assets to mature at the same time as the debt since this means that the project is hedged against changes in interest rates. If you have debts for two and a half years but the project assets run for five years, you may need to refinance in the middle of the project. At this time the interest may be completely different from when you first calculated the financial viability of the project and you may wind up with an unprofitable project.

Growth (in revenues, cash flows and profits) Last year's numbers/this year's equals the growth. Together with WACC and ROIC, it forms the very foundation for all financial value drivers.

Return on invested capital (ROIC) Net operating profits after taxes (NOPAT)/ invested capital = ROIC.

Total free cash flow The amount of cash generated by a company's operations that can be distributed to the lenders and shareholders without decreasing the production capability of the company.

Value added per employee Value added is a measure of the firm's ability to create value. Value added is the value the company adds to its inputs; the difference between the sales price of the finished item or service and the value of the material, time and finance inputs that are needed to make it.

WACC WACC stands for weighted average cost of capital and simply measures the average cost of debt and equity.

Intellectual capital

Application rates from target groups The number of applications the company receives on a yearly basis is an indicator of the company's reputation as an employer. Of course, quality is more important than quantity and therefore you should measure the application rates from the groups that the firm tries to attract in its recruitment efforts.

Competence development expense/employee This is the money spent on developing the specialist skills and knowledge of the employees. This would, for example, mean a seminar on how to do business in Malaysia for the new market officer or a course on C++ programming for dynamic databases for a programmer. This measurement does not contain money spent on increasing general industry knowledge and understanding.

Corporate quality performance (ISO 9002) How much is the company deviating from its quality standards? Is the company ISO 9002 compliant? Is it performing according to ISO 9002 criteria?

Customer brand loyalty index This is one indicator of how well investments in the brand are paying off. How inclined are the customers to change supplier of the good or service in question? How strong a hold does the brand have on its users?

Industry training and education cost Money spent on general education of the industry and its components. An example would be seminars on the next generation of websites for consultants of a web-design firm or an individual from a law firm attending a seminar on the topic of the growing importance of intellectual property law.

Investment in public relations All money spent on building and improving relations with the public. This may be through PR and lobbying firms or through general PR activities.

Investments in brands These are all the investments spent on trying to create, build, strengthen, promote and develop brands. This measurement usually equals the marketing budget minus costs that do not increase the future earning capabilities of brands.

Leadership training and education cost All the money spent on training and educating employees in leadership. Note that this measure includes employees from all ranks, not just management.

Motivation index This index will show how well the investments in internal relations are paying off. How motivated are the employees? This is measured by asking the employees questions such as: How interesting do you find your work? Do you feel motivated?

Revenue-generating staff/total staff Revenue-generating staff is defined as all the employees with a core responsibility to generate revenue for the firm.

Satisfied customer index The number of customers that will claim to be satisfied with the quality of product/service provided. Above one means delivery above expectations. How efficient is the company as a supplier? Are they delivering the quality promised? The quantity? Are they timely? How is the product/service support? The same questions are asked of suppliers to get the supplier efficiency index.

Satisfied employee index This is an indication of how happy the employees are at and with the firm. How satisfied are the employees? How much do they enjoy their work? Are they satisfied with their working environment? Do they feel appreciated and do they appreciate their colleagues?

Supplier efficiency index How efficient are the suppliers? Are they delivering the quality promised? The quantity? Are they timely? How is the product/service support? The same questions are asked of customers to get the customer satisfaction index.

Win/loss index This is the ratio between the customers approached and won and the customers approached and lost. It gives information on the effectiveness of the sales force.

Industry structure

Entry/exit barriers Barriers to entry is the common way of referring to factors that make it more difficult and/or more expensive to establish a presence in an industry.

Industry growth The industry growth can be said to consist of two variables: general GDP growth and industry-specific growth.

Negotiating power of customers Customers with a strong bargaining position can decrease the profitability in an industry by demanding lower prices, better service or better performance.

Negotiating power of suppliers Suppliers can decrease profitability in an industry if they have a strong negotiating position.

Relative market share A company's market share divided by the sum of the market shares of, for example, the four biggest players in the industry. This measure gives a good indication of how dominant a company is in a specific industry as well as of the general level of competition in the industry.

Threat from substitutes A substitute is a product or service fulfilling the same need or function as the good or service in question. Substitute products limit profitability in an industry by setting an upper limit on the price of the product.

Threat/protection from regulations Governments often regulate markets, most often at the cost of the customer and to the benefit of the companies in the industry. Whichever way the regulations might direct the benefits, it needs to be accounted for.

Appendix B

Suggested information needed for a valuation

Industry and competition

A. Market size and characteristics

- Describe each separate geographic market for each of the company's services/product groups (information provided worldwide).
- Set forth any market surveys (or other market information) from independent institutes you have access to.

B. Market trends

- Describe historical, current and future patterns or trends relating to each market (together with reasons why), including:
  - Changes in pricing
  - Changes in customer base
  - Changes in the types of users
  - Forward or backward integration trends.

C. Market structure

- Describe the different categories of participants in each market with detailed descriptions of the major participants.

■ Distinguish between competition from outside the industry and from within the industry, e.g. are larger and financially stronger companies acquiring lines of business in the company's industry?

■ Describe the stability of companies engaged in the industry, e.g. any failures? If so, reasons?

■ Describe the current market share of each major participant.

■ Describe any historical and projected changes in the relative market share of major participants and discuss reasons for these changes.

D. Characteristics of competitors

■ Describe and assess the factors affecting the relative success of each major competitor:

– The existence of any economies of scale enjoyed by the competitor, e.g. in purchasing, marketing or distributing

– The existence of product differentiation enjoyed by the competitor, e.g. premium prices, customer loyalty

– The existence of backward or forward integration enjoyed by the competitor

– The existence of any other advantages enjoyed by the competitor, including:

  – superior management

  – superior facilities

  – superior technological know-how

  – favourable access to attractive workforce

  – favourable relationships with suppliers

  – favourable relationships with customers or customer groups.

■ Describe the ways in which each major competitor competes and other significant behavioural traits of each major competitor, with special attention to the following:

– Price competition

– Service competition

– Trends towards (or away from) concentration or domination

– Niche players? Mavericks?

– Responsible/irresponsible competitors (ethical/legal behaviour, etc.)?

Company specifics

A. Products/services

- Describe historical and projected volume, revenues and expenses attributable to each major product/service, e.g. during past year, most recent interim period and next year.

- Describe any products/services that are presently in development stage, including expected dates of introduction, results of any testing, estimated start-up costs and costs of building facilities, working capital requirements and expected financial results.

- Describe the degree of risk to which the company is exposed in terms of technological substitution, obsolescence, etc. and in the event of termination of exclusive proprietary rights.

B. Overview of cost structure

- Describe each major component of cost-of-sales, e.g. the total and relative amount of labour costs, direct overhead costs, etc. Describe how (and why) these component costs have changed, on a relative and absolute basis, over time.

- Provide a detailed list of direct general, selling and administrative expenses attributable to each individual major product/service.

- Provide explanations for any positive or negative trends in sales, gross profit or selling and administrative expense ratios, by product/service.

C. Suppliers

- Which products/services are and will be developed in-house and which are and will be acquired from suppliers?

- Describe the suppliers.

- Describe the terms of any long-term supply contracts between the company and a supplier or any other major commitments of the company regarding the purchase of raw materials.

- Describe the terms and conditions of the company's relationship with major suppliers.

D. Research and development

■ Describe the company's R&D activities, including historical and projected R&D expenditures and facilities.

■ Describe the focus/strategy of the company's R&D activities, e.g. primarily improvements/enhancements of existing products/services or the development of new products?

■ Describe how the company's R&D activities compare with industry averages.

E. Quality control

■ Describe the company's system(s) for maintaining/improving the quality of its products, e.g. the number of personnel involved in quality control and their background and expertise; inspection, testing and other activities undertaken, etc.

Marketing

A. Customer base

■ Describe the customer base of the company, including prototypical traits of the average customer. Is the customer base divided into subgroups today?

■ Describe historical and projected changes in the customer base of the company together with the reasons for such changes.

■ Provide a descriptive list of the company's key customers, including:

– Sales

– Loyalty

– Contractual arrangement.

■ Indicate the number and/or identity of customers that account for a significant percentage of the company's sales.

B. Marketing organization

■ Describe the marketing organization employed by the company, including marketing personnel, organizational structure, incentive arrangements and the use of outside marketing expertise.

C. Advertising and promotion

▓ Compare the company's marketing efforts and budgets with those of major competitors.

▓ Describe marketing strategies recently adopted and/or discontinued (and reasons why).

▓ Describe the importance of each of the following to the company's marketing efforts:

  – Product differentiation (brand, name, quality image, technological or other superiority)

  – Pricing (does the company sell at a premium or discount to competitive products?)

  – Favoured customer relationships

  – Servicing.

D. Pricing policies

▓ Describe how prices are set, and by whom.

▓ Describe any price supports or trade barriers enjoyed by the company or any of its competitors.

Sales profile

A. Sales organization

▓ Describe the sales force employed by the company, including personnel, organizational structure and incentive arrangements.

▓ Describe any training provided to the company's sales force.

▓ Describe any outside sales organizations used by the company, including compensation arrangements, markets served, volume and revenue of product distributed by each, duration of the relationship and degree of satisfaction.

▓ Describe all channels of distribution used by the company, including volume and sales attributable to each.

▓ Describe any significant historical and projected behaviour and trends concerning methods of sales and distribution used by the company and the industry generally.

B. Sales trends

▪ Describe historical, current and future sales trends, including seasonality of sales, cycles and geographical distribution.

C. Foreign sales and operations

▪ Describe historical, current and projected revenues and profits, e.g. during past year, most recent interim period and next year, attributable to foreign operations or sales, including country-by-country breakdown together with a description of the reasons for any trends or changes.

▪ Describe any special risks attending to these sales or operations.

▪ Describe effects of changing exchange rates, if any.

D. Sales returns and allowances

▪ Provide an analysis of sales returns and allowances for the past three years and for the most recent interim period, together with an explanation for any unusual amounts, trends or changes.

Employees

▪ Describe the total number of employees and their average number of months with the company.

▪ Break out the number of the company's employees as follows:

  – By geographic location (if the company has more than one facility)

  – By type of employment (full-time vs part-time)

  – By union workers vs non-union workers

  – By compensation arrangement

  – By function or expertise, e.g. the number of sales personnel, the number of personnel in office administration, the number of personnel involved in the actual production of product, etc.

▪ Describe each of the company's employee benefit plans, e.g. pension, bonus, health, accident, life insurance, stock option, and retirement plans.

▪ Describe the company's employee compensation arrangements, and assess whether they are competitive.

■ Describe any outside consultants and/or freelance workers retained from time to time by the company, including:

– Tasks performed

– Compensation arrangements

– Reasons for not using in-house employees.

Historical financial information

A. Historical income statements

■ Set forth the company's income statements for the past fiscal year and for the most recent interim period (and corresponding period of preceding year).

■ Where the company's sales are carried out in distinctive geographic markets, provide the income statement information above by geographic region.

B. Historical balance sheet

Set forth the company's balance sheets for the past fiscal year and for the most recent interim period (and corresponding period of preceding year).

C. Historical statements of operating cash flow

Set forth the company's statements of operating cash flow for the past fiscal year and for the most recent interim period (and corresponding period of preceding year).

D. Notes to financial statements

Describe, in detail, each adjustment that either has already been made or is appropriate to make in order to reflect the actual financial performance and condition of the company, including:

– The exclusion of dividends paid

– The exclusion of management fees paid

– The exclusion of any operations that were not or are not part of the company to be divested

- The exclusion of any corporate overhead allocated to but not incurred by company

- The elimination of all intra-company receivables and/or payments

- Any corresponding adjustments to income tax and depreciation

- The elimination of any non-recurring extraordinary item.

■ Describe significant accounting policies used by the company including those relating to:

- Valuation of inventories, e.g. FIFO, LIFO, average, retail inventory, base stock

- Depreciation, e.g. straight line, years, machine hours, units produced, sum of years digit, double declining, sinking fund

- Provision for pension costs, e.g. actuarial methods and assumptions used, funding methods used and unfunded past or prior service costs and the relationship of funded amounts to vested benefits

- Research and development costs, e.g. charged directly to expense or amortized over a period of years. Also accounting for internally developed intangible assets

- Realization of income:

  - sale of products/services (at time of sale, upon collection of sales price, or completion of products)

  - sales to affiliated type companies

  - cash discounts taken by customers on sales and effect on income, e.g. at time of sale or at time of collection

- Unamortized discount and expenses on debt or refunded debt, e.g. straight line or interest method of amortization

- Accounting for self-insurance, e.g. reserved or expensed as incurred

- Accounting for foreign exchange translation gains and losses

- Consolidation policies, e.g. full consolidation, equity or cost

- Bases of valuation of long-term investments

- Accounting for material leases of property, e.g. capitalized or expensed

- The method of carrying investments in the financial statements.

- Provide detailed information concerning all extraordinary credits and charges.

- Provide detailed information concerning accruals for contingent liabilities, litigation, warranties under contracts and foreign currency losses.

Financial projections

A. The company's projected income statement for the next three years

- Set forth a detailed, projected income statement of the company for each of the next three years. As far as possible, use the same accounting methods and line items that are used in the company's historical and current income statements. To the extent that there is any deviation, explain the reason(s) for the deviation and provide reconciliations where possible.

- Make liberal use of footnotes to cross-refer from the projected income statement to the assumptions section, which should accompany the financial projections.

B. Specialized projected income statements for the next three years

- Where the company offers multiple, distinct products/services or product lines, prepare projected income statements by product line to include the information set out in Paragraph A above.

- Where the company's sales are carried out in distinct geographic markets, prepare projected income statements, broken out by geographic region, to include the information set out in Paragraph A above.

C. The company's projected balance sheets for the next three years

- Set forth a detailed, projected balance sheet of the company for each of the next three years. As far as possible, use the same accounting methods and line items that are used in the company's historical and current balance sheets. To the extent that there is any deviation, explain the reason(s) for the deviation and provide reconciliations where possible.

- Make liberal use of footnotes to cross-refer from the projected balance sheets to the assumptions section, which should accompany the financial projections.

D. The company's projected operating cash flow for the next three years

▨ Set forth a detailed, projected operating cash flow for the company for each of the next three years. As far as possible, use the same accounting methods and line items that are used in the company's historical and current statements of operating cash flows. To the extent that there is any deviation, explain the reason(s) for the deviation and provide reconciliations where possible.

E. Assumptions to financial projections

▨ Set forth the growth rate, implied or assumed, for each component of projected revenues. Quantify the extent to which an increase/decrease in a growth rate is attributable to an increase/decrease in price and/or is attributable to an increase/decrease in volume. Briefly explain the reason(s) for any increase or decrease.

▨ Set forth the growth rate, implied or assumed, for the company's assets, liabilities and equity. Explain the reason(s) for any increase/decrease or large investments or divestments.

▨ Describe in detail all assumptions made (and the reasons why) regarding each of the following:

- The rate of inflation over the projected three-year period

- The company's tax rate for each of the three years

- Where foreign sales or income are significant, the exchange rates in effect over the projected three-year period

- Interest rates applicable to the company's debt (if any) over the projected three-year period

- The capital structure and financing of the company over the projected three-year period, e.g. the amount of debt incurred or retired, the amount of equity issued or retired, etc.

- Dividend payments over the projected three-year period

- Any change in accounting policies over the projected three-year period

- Any significant non-recurring or extraordinary income or expense implied or assumed, e.g. the acquisition or sale of any material assets, and the quantitative impact of any other extraordinary event within the company's operations or the market(s) at large.

Glossary

Book value The shareholders' value that is recorded on the balance sheet. This value is also the book value of the shareholders' part of the assets. The book value rarely agrees with the market valuation of the company equity.

CAGR Compound annual growth rate. The year-over-year return or growth over a specific number of years. Used to estimate what the return or growth would have been if it was the same every year during the period.

Continuing value or terminal value The discounted value of all free cash flows for the period after the explicit value period (and the hypergrowth period if this is used) to infinity.

COGS Cost of goods sold. This represents the cost of buying raw material and producing finished goods. It includes precise costs (for example, materials and labour) and variable costs (such as factory overheads).

CRM Customer relationship management. An information industry term for methodologies, software, and internet capabilities that help a company manage customer relationships in an organized way.

DCF Discounted cash flow. A valuation method whereby future cash flows are discounted to a present value at an appropriate interest rate.

Debt/equity ratio Gives information on how much debt the company has in relation to its shareholders' equity. Arrived at by dividing the company's debts by its shareholders' equity.

Depreciation The part of an investment that is recorded as a cost in a given year and that therefore has an impact on that year's earnings.

Discount rate The rate by which a given cash flow is multiplied. In a DCF calculation this figure is always below 1 and comprises $1/(1 + \text{WACC})$ powered by the number of years that are to be discounted.

Earnings The balance of revenue after deduction of costs and expenses.

EBIT Earnings before interest and tax. A financial measure defined as revenues less cost of goods sold and selling, general, and administrative expenses. In other words, operating and non-operating profit before the deduction of interest and income taxes.

EBITDA Earnings before interest and tax, depreciation and amortization, but after all product/service, sales and overhead (SG&A) costs are accounted for. Sometimes referred to as operating profit.

ECE Estimated cost of equity. A simplified method for calculating the cost of equity.

Explicit value period The period that concerns the next few years for which it is possible to predict cash flows with reasonable accuracy and during which free cash flows are calculated for each individual year.

FIFO First in, first out. An inventory cost flow whereby the first goods purchased are assumed to be the first goods sold so that the ending inventory consists of the most recently purchased goods.

Free cash flow Cash flow that is available to all of the company's financiers and other claimants.

Hypergrowth period A number of years after the explicit period during which a company's cash flows grow faster than during 'steady state' but during which it is not worthwhile calculating the cash flows explicitly.

Industry structure Refers to the competitive structure of the industry in which the company operates. The competitiveness of an industry is often measured through rivalry, barriers to entry, negotiating power of the suppliers, negotiating power of the customers and threat from substitutes.

Intellectual capital The value of a company's aggregate knowledge, experience, organizational technology, professional competence and customer relations. Intellectual capital is often divided into human and structural capital.

Key value driver A variable that has a significant impact on the value of an asset.

LBO Leveraged buyout. In an LBO, the acquiring party finances the deal predominantly through loans (i.e. has a very high debt/equity ratio) that are then repaid with the cash flow from the acquired company. Became very popular in the 1980s when Michael Milken provided large and relatively cheap volumes of loan financing through the invention of 'junk bonds'.

LIFO Last in, first out. An inventory cost flow whereby the last goods purchased are assumed to be the first goods sold so that the ending inventory consists of the first purchased goods.

MBO Management buyout. Similar to a leveraged buyout, but the acquiring party is led by the management of the company being acquired.

Multiple A multiple reflects the value of the company in relation to a specific variable. For example, a revenue multiple reflects the value of the enterprise in relation to its revenues.

Net asset valuation The difference between the assets and liabilities taken from the balance sheet and adjusted for accounting entries that should not affect the value.

NOPLAT Net operating profit less adjusted tax. A company's potential cash earnings if its capitalization was unleveraged (that is, if it had no debt). NOPLAT is frequently used in economic value added (EVA) calculations.

PPE Property, plant and equipment. A balance sheet item. The original cost of assets, less their accumulated depreciation. Often called fixed assets.

SGA Selling, general and administrative expense. Reported on the income statement, it includes all costs associated with selling and general expenses of running the business.

Steady state When the company's growth can be assumed to be constant at approximately the level of general GDP growth. This is also the last phase of a company's growth development and is used as the starting point for the terminal value period.

Venture capital Early-stage corporate financing.

WACC Weighted average cost of capital. Companies are generally financed by a combination of debt and equity. The WACC is the average cost of these sources of company finance.

WC Working capital. Comprises the aggregate value of liquid cash, customer relations, inventory minus accounts payable and interest-free current liabilities.

Further reading

Reports and books

The Balanced Scorecard, R. Kaplan and D. Norton, Boston, Harvard Business School Press, 1996.

Buffettology: The previously unexplained techniques that have made Warren Buffett the world's most famous investor, M. Buffett and D. Clark, Simon & Schuster, 1997.

Competing for the Future, G. Hamel and C. K. Prahalad, Boston, Harvard Business School Press, 1994.

Competitive Strategy – Techniques for Analyzing Industries and Competitors, M. E. Porter, Boston, The Free Press, 1980 and 1998.

Creating Shareholder Value, A. Rappaport, Simon & Schuster, 1998.

Essays in Company Valuation, Joakim Levin, doctoral dissertation, Stockholm, Stockholm School of Economics, 1998.

EVA and Value Based Management – A Practical Guide to Implementation, S. D. Young and S. F. O'Byrne, McGraw-Hill Education, 2001.

Funky Business – Talent Makes Capital Dance, K. A. Nordström and J. Ridderstråle, Financial Times Prentice Hall, 2000.

The Gorilla Game – An Investors' Guide to Picking Winners in Hi-technology, G. A. Moore, P. Johnson and T. Kippola, Capstone Publishing Limited, 1998.

Intellectual Capital – Navigating in the New Business Landscape, J. Roos, G. Roos, L. Edvinsson and N. Dragonetti, Basingstoke, Palgrave, 1997.

Intellectual Capital – The Proven Way to Establish your Company's Real Value by Measuring its Hidden Brain Power, L. Edvinsson and M. Malone, HarperBusiness, 1997.

Principles of Corporate Finance, R. Brealy and S. Meyers, Higher Education US Editions, McGraw-Hill, 1996.

Real Options – A Practioner's Guide, T. Copeland and V. Antikarov, Texere Publishing, 2000.

The Quest for Value, G.B. Stewart III, HarperCollins, 1991.

Valuation of Companies in Emerging Markets, L. E. Pereiro, John Wiley & Sons, 2002.

Valuation of Knowledge Companies – Identifying the Key Value Drivers, D. Frykman and J. Tolleryd, IVA – Royal Swedish Academy of Engineering Sciences, 1999.

Valuation – Measuring and Managing the Value of Companies, 3rd edition, T. Copeland, T. Coller and J. Murrin, John Wiley & Sons, 1995.

Value Based Management – The Corporate Response to the Shareholder Revolution, J. D. Martin and J.W. Petty, Oxford University Press Inc., 2000.

Valuing Financial Institutions, Z. C. Mercer, McGraw-Hill Education, 1992.

Articles

A better tool for valuing operations, T. Luehrman, *Harvard Business Review,* May–June 1997.

Dividend policy, growth and the valuation of shares, F. Modigliani and M. Miller, *Journal of Business,* Vol. 34:4, 1961.

Terminal value techniques in equity valuation – implications of the steady state assumption, J. Levin and P. Olsson, *SSE/EFI Working Paper Series in Business Administration*, No. 2000:7, 2000.

The cost of capital, corporation finance and the theory of investment, F. Modigliani and M. Miller, *American Economic Review*, Vol. 48:3, 1958.

The pricing of options and corporate liabilities, F. Black and M. Scholes, *Journal of Political Economy*, 1973.

The real power of real options, K. Leslie and M. Michaels, *McKinsey Quarterly*, No. 3, 1997.

What's it worth? A general manager's guide to valuation, T. Luehrman, *Harvard Business Review*, May–June 1997.

Index

Comprehensive. Authoritative. Trusted.

FT Guides will tell you everything you need to know about your chosen subject area

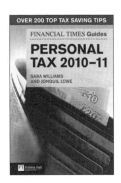

9780273735694

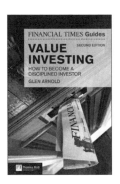

9780273724520

9780273722014

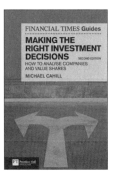

9780273729846

9780273712671

9780273723967

9780273727835

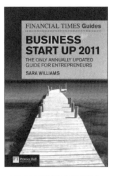

9780273740568

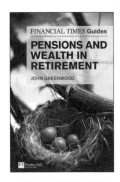

9780273727859

9780273723745

9780273727873

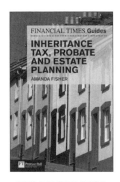

9780273729969

Change your business life today

FT Prentice Hall
FINANCIAL TIMES